MAXPOINT

Your Journey to Maximum Significance

Frank Banfill

Kay Adam
PUBLISHING

Published by Kay Adam Publishing, Wylie, Texas
www.KayAdamBooks.com

Printed in the United States of America

Library of Congress Control Number: 2005910483

ISBN 0-9776532-0-X

Contents

Preface

A funny thing happened while I wrote this book: it changed my life. I didn't intend for it to, but it did.

Billy Graham said that he was always the first person to respond to his famous invitations to come forward at the end of his sermon, except he didn't respond in the stadium where he preached, but beforehand in his room as he prepared each of his messages. Maybe that is what happened with me.

As I asked myself the question that I pose in chapter eight "What is your *maxpoint*?" I began to clearly see the answer. I also realized that if I stayed where I was at, doing what I was doing, I would never reach it. Don't get me wrong: what I was doing at the time was good, very good. But good, however, is the greatest threat to "great." When we settle for something good, we miss out on something great.

I had been right in the center of God's will and His hand was blessing my work. But God made it clear that He had something new for me. I would need to make another step of faith in the continuing journey towards my *maxpoint*.

Wherever you find yourself in the journey of life, I believe the solid principles that you will find in these pages will help you take that next step to becoming everything that you were created to become. Young, old, or in between, as long as you have breath, God desires to work in and through you. God has something incredible in store for your life, and I believe this book can help you find it.

I have had the privilege of visiting more than two dozen countries. I've met people from all walks of life, social levels, and economic statuses. I've seen people at various stages of life who merely survive life—and I have seen those who thrive. I am convinced that most people will never reach their full potential. It is not that they can't, rather, it is more like they won't. Some won't because they don't understand how; others won't because they make poor choices. I don't want you to be in either of those groups! I want you to experience the best of life. I want you to find significance—the kind of significance that outlasts your life. More importantly, God wants this for you. He wants you to reach your destiny, which is the very reason why He created you. He wants you to thrive in life. So, buckle your seatbelt and let's get ready for your journey to maximum significance!

Acknowledgements

There have been so many people who have impacted my life over the years. They have been at just the right place at just the right time to help me take the next step in personal and professional development. Teachers, professors, pastors and colleagues have all played a vital part in my journey. I am thankful to these people, the congregation I used to pastor, and the many people who have accompanied me on international mission trips over the years. Each one has taught me something important about life.

I want to especially thank Bobb Biehl for his wisdom, counsel, and for suggesting the title to this book. Thanks to Gregg Wooding for conducting interviews and helping write some of the stories in chapter eight. I also want to thank Burt Barrett and Doug Waymire for their edits to my original draft.

Finally, words cannot express my appreciation and love for my wife Beth. When we were married in 1991, she promised to "support me in all of my endeavors." She has definitely done that over the years. Thanks, Sweetheart, for believing in me and challenging me to be my best.

Chapter 1
The Journey to the Point

There were millions of people who, like me, sat on the edge of their seats watching television on February 6, 1982. We were watching *ABC's Wide World of Sports* and its coverage of a then-obscure event called the Ironman Triathlon. What kept us mesmerized on that Saturday afternoon wasn't the event itself, but rather the performance of one of its athletes.

The Ironman is one of the most grueling endurance competitions in the world. It involves swimming 2.4 miles, bicycling 112 miles, and then running 26.2 miles — all in one day. The competition took place in Hawaii, and would come to be known as the event that would popularize and forever change the sport. On that day, the Ironman became famous, thanks to a 23-year-old college student named Julie Moss.

Unlike many participants in the extreme competition, Julie was not a seasoned athlete trying to prove something. She simply was looking for an excuse to vacation in Hawaii under the guise of researching a college project.[1] Julie paid the $85 entry fee and joined 580 other people in

---

[1] Source: Ironman Triathlon website http://vnews.ironmanlive .com/vnews//1044381287/?keywords=julie:moss.

the competition.[2] However, no one really noticed Julie that day until the competition neared the end.

Julie did well in the ocean swim and on the bike, and found herself leading the women in the marathon. As she continued along, she began to get that champion drive inside of her – "You can do this! You can do this! Not only can you finish it, but you can win this thing!"

But as she pushed on through those grueling miles her body began to weaken. The run became a quick gait which turned to a slow walk. A clearly fatigued Julie lost control of her bodily functions.

As hundreds of onlookers gathered to cheer her on and multitudes more of us watched at home, she collapsed just yards from the finish line. But Julie would not quit. She got down on her hands and knees and literally crawled to the finish line. Despite her gallant efforts, Julie lost the women's competition by just 29 seconds to another runner named Kathleen McCartney.[3] Even though she came in second, Julie was victorious because she crossed the finish line. She gave the Ironman Triathlon unprecedented fame and birthed the concept "just finishing an Ironman is a victory."

All of us are in a grueling marathon. It is a marathon much bigger than the Ironman. It is the marathon called life. It is a journey that takes us over rugged mountains and through winding valleys, into the deep green

---

[2] Source: http://vnews.ironmanlive.com/vnews//1042568588/?keywords=julie:moss.

[3] Source: http://vnews.ironmanlive.com/vnews//1048622677/?keywords=julie:moss.

meadows and across barren deserts. The problem with many of us is that we do not understand the goal of our journey.

You see, many people view their journey like Julie Moss' triathlon—all that matters is that you somehow, some way, make it across the finish line. The finish line is defined as the end of our life and the entrance into Heaven if you are a believer in Christ. They see the journey as all about getting to Heaven. Thus, according to them, the purpose of life is to hang on as best you can until you reach the glorious "by and by."

I would submit to you that this view is not only a faulty understanding of Scripture, but it is a lie that Satan is using to paralyze the Body of Christ. When you accepted Jesus Christ as your Savior—assuming you've made that decision—your eternal destiny was sealed. You are as much in Heaven as if you were standing there today. My assurance of eternal life with God in Heaven is not based on anything I do. It is not based on my ability to make it through this life. It is not about coming to the end of my life and seeing if my good works outweigh the bad. No, our eternal destiny is based on what Jesus Christ has done for us and whether or not we have appropriated His forgiveness for our sins.

Our life journey is about something much more than being a survivor. The journey is about reaching our *maxpoint*. This point is the place in our lives where we are maximizing our gifts, abilities, talents, experiences— everything that we are—for God's glory. It is the place where our lives are making the biggest impact possible for the Kingdom of God. Julie Moss made a great impact on sports. God wants to use us in even greater ways to impact the world and bring incredible glory to Himself.

I want you to grab a piece of paper and a pen. On the top-third of your paper, draw a little dot. Now circle it. This circle represents your *destiny* and the dot in the center represents your *maxpoint*, the place where you are maximizing your life for the greatest Kingdom impact.

Now on the bottom-third of your page, draw another circle. This time, instead of a dot in the center, draw arrows going out from the edge of the circle in several directions.

Here's the problem: most Christians don't operate inside the first circle like they should. Instead, they resemble the second circle. They have no clear direction and their lives spin somewhat aimlessly. Oh, they go to church each week. They may teach a Bible study, tithe or even serve in church leadership, but they are not on a trajectory that will take them to their *maxpoint*.

They are bumping along, feeling their way through life, trying to make it to what they think is the finish line. What they don't realize is that God has so much more for them than they are experiencing. They may be growing incrementally in their faith as a result of some exposure to the Word of God, but they're not fully engaged in the Kingdom like God desires. Their thoughts are consumed with what is happening in their lives each day and not how they can maximize their lives for God's glory. Even those of us who are in the so-called "ministry" can fall into this trap.

As we begin to think about the journey God wants to take us on, let's look at the journey embarked on by a fellow named Abraham. The Bible says in Genesis 11: 31-12:3,

> *"Terah took his son Abram, his grandson Lot, son of Haran, and his daughter-in-law Sarai, the wife of his son Abram, and together they set out from Ur of the Chaldeans to go to Canaan. But when they came to Haran, they settled there. Terah lived 205 years, and he died in Haran. The Lord had said to Abram, 'Leave your country, your people and your father's household and go to the land I will show you.'"*

It is interesting to note that Abram, whose name was later changed to Abraham by God, originally started his journey towards Canaan, which is where the Lord wanted him. It was in Canaan where Abraham would eventually reach his *maxpoint*. Likewise, when we come to faith in Jesus Christ, God starts us on a journey towards our *maxpoint*.

Notice, however, what Abraham did. He started toward Canaan but, for some reason, settled down along the way. He quit far short of where God wanted him. This is an epidemic problem with today's believers: we stop short of where God wants us. We are on this journey, heading toward our *maxpoint*, but for some reason, we settle down far short of God's intended destination.

I witness this phenomenon constantly as my work in missions takes me to numerous churches around the world. The monologue goes something like this: "Boy, I would love to be a missionary. I would love to travel and share Jesus with people. In fact, when I was a teenager, I believed God was calling me to be a missionary. But then I got out of high school, went to college, got a job and *settled down*."

The world is full of believers who have settled down. They are supposed to be on this great journey, but they've stopped. What have they settled into? They've settled into a comfort zone, which is probably the greatest threat to reaching our *maxpoint.*

It has been said that a comfort zone is really nothing more than a prison cell with felt-covered bars. Think what it would be like inside a cell. Now, imagine you are in solitary confinement. You are in "the hole." You know there is a world out there, but you can't see it. You can't see the sunshine, and you can't see what's happening in the world because you are in confinement. That is exactly the way our comfort zone works. We get locked into it, and it keeps us from experiencing the world that God has for us. God is doing incredible things out there and we will miss it if we stay locked in our comfort zone.

God said to Abraham in Genesis 12:1,

> *"I want you to leave your country, leave your people, leave your father's household and go to a land I will show you."*

Notice from this that there are three things that comprise our comfort zone. The first is location.

God said to Abraham, "Leave your country." That is his location, the geographical area where he lived. God called him out of the place where he had settled. We often settle into a particular location and will not even entertain the thought of leaving it. God, however, says that we need to be willing to move outside of our location—outside of our comfort zone—in order to experience what He has for us in other places.

One of the people God used to alert me to the fact I was in a geographic comfort zone was a Romanian pastor named Iosif Tson. Tson is an incredible man of God. He pastored a large Baptist church during the days of Communism and was regularly persecuted for his faith. The authorities threatened him with death if he continued preaching. His response to them was, "Please, do it! The greatest thing you could do is to kill me because if you kill me you make me a martyr, and that will only energize Christianity in Romania." As you can imagine, they didn't kill him. Eventually, he was able to travel outside of Romania and that is when I first heard him speak. I was a college freshman when Tson spoke at my Christian university's annual missions conference.

As Tson and others spoke during that conference, the Spirit of God began to convict my heart. At the age of 12, I surrendered my life to the ministry. I felt that God was calling me to be an evangelist, to travel across the United States and call people to Christ. I was attending a Christian university to prepare to do just that. Although I never verbalized it, it was as if I had said, "God, I'll go anywhere you want me to go and do anything you want me to do just as long as it is between Maine and California, Florida and Alaska."

I thought that was pretty good. I was willing to go anywhere in America, and, after all, America is a big place. At least that is what I thought at the time. I never thought about the world outside of America. Actually, I really didn't know that there was a world outside of America. Sure, I had studied about the world in school, and from time to time, I would even take note of international news;

but for all practical purposes the United States *was* the world.

My world changed one of those nights at that missions conference. I responded to the invitation given by another speaker that week, Ed Dobson, to come forward and make a global commitment. I remember getting down on my knees and saying to God, "Lord, I will go *anywhere* in the world you want me to go. I will do *anything* you want me to do. Wherever you lead, I will follow." Next to my salvation, that was probably the greatest decision I've ever made in my life. That prayer effectively unlocked the cell door of my geographical comfort zone. That commitment made it easy to decide to go on a university-sponsored mission trip to Australia three years later. It was on that trip I met the young woman who would later become my wife, another student who had answered the call.

Thanks to the decision to abandon that comfort zone, I not only met my wife, but I have had the incredible privilege to travel the world and see God at work. I have seen Him move in ways that I never would have if I had stayed in my little location, my little comfort zone. Not only that, but I have seen God do things *through me* that otherwise would not have been possible.

Comfort zones are funny things. Just because you move out of one, it does not mean that you are home free. In fact, all throughout the journey to our *maxpoint*, these comfort zones keep popping up. They are like rest areas along interstate highways. You see them every so many miles, and eventually turn into one. Now, there is nothing wrong with rest areas. They serve an important function—

just as long as they are a pause along the journey and not a permanent stop.

I used to pastor in a city of 26,000 people. We lived in a neighboring city and each day that I drove to the church, I would pass a sign that said, "Welcome to North Ridgeville. Population 26,000." As I did, I would cry out to God, "Lord, give us North Ridgeville for you." It was a noble prayer, but one that needed to be balanced with the bigger picture. You see, just because I had moved out of one comfort zone it did not mean that I was not susceptible to another one. If I wasn't careful, I was in danger of shrinking my world to the size of North Ridgeville.

Now don't misunderstand: pleading for the salvation of the city where God had placed us was a *good* thing. It was right to cry out to God for the souls of those 26,000 people. It was right to lead the congregation to share the gospel aggressively with as many residents as possible. It was part of the heart and will of God. But it was not the *only* thing on God's heart. There were more than six billion people who were also on God's heart. Tim Dearborn says it well when he writes, "It is not the Church of God that has a mission in this world, but rather the God of mission who has a church in the world." My role as a pastor was to lead my church to "discover and develop its Great Commission assignment," which is how Sam Ingrassia of Global Missions Fellowship phrases it. My job was to direct our church to fit into God's mission.

In addition to geography, there are two more comfort zones outlined in God's directive to Abraham. One is the cultural comfort zone. Culture is more than our language, food, and mannerisms. It really is everything about us. It is our job. It is the people with whom we like to spend time. It is our economic status and many other things. Let's face it: many of us are trapped in a cultural comfort zone that we don't want to move out of because, well, it is so comfortable.

My first mission trip was to the country of Papua New Guinea, an island nation north of Australia. I flew into the capital city of Port Moresby and then to the interior to a city called Mt. Hagen. When I landed, I was greeted by the American missionary friends with whom I would work. It was well past lunchtime and I hadn't eaten, so we stopped at a restaurant. The food was served cafeteria style. My missionary friend said, "Pick whatever you want." I looked at the "food" before me. *Pick whatever I want*, I said to myself, *I'm not sure what this stuff is. It may start moving any minute. I don't know if I want to do this.* At that moment, I experienced culture shock. I was in a strange place, where they had just discovered clothes shortly before my arrival, I was being invited to eat strange food, and on top of that, they didn't speak English. I had no clue how to function in such a place. My cultural comfort zone had definitely been shattered!

Cross-cultural experiences are not limited to distant travel. I once preached at a rescue mission in downtown Los Angeles, right on "skid row." I wasn't in a foreign country, but I surely was in a foreign culture. Though just miles from where I was born, I had to move out of *my* culture in order to minister there. I was in the presence of men, women, and even children who made their beds on the street. These were people who lived in another world;

a world that many Americans drive past each day without realizing it exists.

Those people were listening to me preach for one reason (and no, it wasn't because they wanted to hear my "great words of wisdom"). They were there simply to get lunch. The rescue mission required them to sit through a service before they could eat. Once they got to the food, they stood at a tall table. There was not enough space to accommodate everyone eating simultaneously, so they moved through the feeding line quickly to give others a chance to eat. I was experiencing a different culture and I hadn't even left my home state.

There is another comfort zone God wants us to venture from called *our family*. God said to Abraham, "I want you to leave your father's house," which included his extended family. In essence, God was saying, "I want you to leave your support group. I want you to let go of people that you have been relying on and step out on this journey with Me." This is a difficult task for many people. After all, we need each other, and support systems are important. We cannot, however, place our ultimate dependency upon our support network, whether it is our family or close friends. Our dependency must first be on God and recognition that it is He who brings people into our lives to help meet our emotional and physical needs. We must be willing to allow God to move us, if He chooses, away from one support group and place us in another. We must trust that God has our best interest at heart.

This lesson hit home for my wife Beth and I, when we sensed God's direction to leave the church I was pastoring in Ohio and move to Texas to join the staff of a missions organization. The Dallas-based international missions agency sought to plant new churches by mobilizing North American and international churches. Granted, we were only moving partway across the United States and not to another country—like so many of our friends had done. Yet, for us it was still a challenge. One of Beth's three brothers lived just three miles from us. Her parents and her other two brothers lived an hour away. Besides her family, there were three other "biggies" that Beth wrestled with as we made the decision to move. There was her job, which she loved and excelled at, her friends, and our church—all of which were part of our support network ... not to mention that there are bugs in Texas—BIG bugs! Add to all of this the fact that I had no guaranteed salary from the missions agency—like many missionaries, we would have to raise financial support to live.

We stepped out, and God was faithful to meet our every need. We had been in Texas about six months when it became clear that God was giving us a new support network, a "surrogate family." We were driving home from church one Sunday afternoon when Beth commented that even if our organization decided to open an office in Ohio and ask me to lead it, she would not want to go back. She was now very happy in Texas. Several years later, there are still things that we miss about Ohio, but God has faithfully enabled us to adapt. He has broadened our experiences and brought many wonderful people into our lives.

We don't know a lot about Abraham's family or how supportive they were of his move. We do know he took his nephew with him. Sometimes, our struggles with the family comfort zone exist because our family is discouraging us from seeking God's will. How many times do we inadvertently keep our family members from becoming all that God wants them to be simply because we selfishly try to hold on to them? I wonder how many parents are going to stand before God in judgment and have to answer for discouraging their children away from the calling that He placed upon their hearts. Beth and I were blessed to have Christian families that encouraged us to follow God's leading. I remember how I broke the news of our impending move to Beth's family, with great apprehension. It was Thanksgiving Day, and the family was gathered at my in-laws' house. I had just flown back that morning after three days of exploratory meetings with the missions agency's leadership team. I waited to make the big announcement until after the turkey was eaten, the pumpkin pie had settled, and the football games ended. After the initial shock and barrage of questions, it was clear that we had the family's full support. Many others, however, are not as fortunate as we were to have such an understanding family.

These comfort zones are a threat to the journey and they can be difficult to overcome, but rest assured that the journey is worth the struggle. This journey brings incredible blessings. In fact, the journey *itself* is a blessing. The Genesis 12 passage goes on to say,

> *"I will make you into a great nation and I will bless you; I will make your name great, and you will be a blessing. I will bless those who bless you, and whoever curses you I will curse; and all peoples on earth will be blessed through you."*

This passage is part of what is known as the Abrahamic Covenant, given specifically to Abraham and his descendents. Although this does not apply directly to Gentile believers, there is a principle here that is repeated elsewhere in Scripture which does apply. As we venture on this journey toward our *maxpoint*, God will bring blessings into our lives and He will cause us to be a blessing to others.

Stop for a moment and think about the people God has used to bless your life. Now thank Him for those people. The flipside of the blessing coin is that God also uses you to bless others. The Apostle Paul put it this way in his first letter to the Thessalonians,

> *"For what is our hope, our joy, or the crown in which we will glory the presence of our Lord Jesus when He comes? Is it not you? Indeed you are our glory and joy." (2:19-20).*

Paul was a blessing to the Thessalonians. He won them to Christ, he discipled them, and he poured his life into them, which in turn blessed him. Do you want to know how meaningful your life is? Look to see how many lives you are impacting. Who are you touching, influencing, and discipling for Christ? You don't know if the next person you lead to Christ and disciple might become the next great evangelist, missionary or pastor. What joy it is to touch positively the lives of others! Truly we are blessed as we minister to people. We can take heart that the journey is worth the effort. God told Abraham in Genesis 15:1, "Do not be afraid, Abram. I am your shield, your very great reward." Payday is coming. There is a blessing that God will give us if we will be faithful to the journey.

Think about it ...

What is the goal of your life right now?

Do you know for sure where you will spend eternity when you die? *Note: If you are not sure that you are headed to Heaven, you can call 1-888-NEED-HIM toll free in the U.S. to talk to someone about how you can have a personal relationship with Jesus Christ. You can also visit their website at www.needhim.org.*

Are you locked into a comfort zone? If so, what is it?

Chapter 2
Stages in the Journey

One of the greatest displays of power and force occurs when the space shuttle is launched. When the engines ignite, it looks like a bomb has been dropped as smoke mushrooms out, a sight visible for many miles. Then, in a seemingly slow and majestic manner, the shuttle begins to lift off from its launch pad as it starts its journey to space.

In many ways, the Christian life is like a shuttle mission. Earlier, we said that many Christians resemble the circle with arrows going a myriad of ways. They do not have a clear direction and certainly are not on a trajectory that would lead to their *maxpoint*. But how does one stop the aimless wandering and lock onto his or her God-given assignment? If they are on the journey, how do they know how to move to the next part of this adventure? What does this journey look like anyway?

There are many parallels between the journey to our *maxpoint* and the shuttle's journey. We, as well as the shuttle, move through various stages until our mission is accomplished. Every shuttle mission begins with the decision that it is necessary. Once that occurs, all of the people, tools, equipment, and resources necessary for the mission are assembled. NASA's will to accomplish the mission is demonstrated by its preparatory actions. The crew is assembled with clear instructions about the purpose, scope, and length of its mission. Crew members undergo many months of intense training. Engineers, technicians, and scientists are gathered. Finally, the shuttle is sitting on its launch pad, with the crew on board awaiting lift off. We will call this part of the mission the *Decision Stage*, which is the period leading up to the launch. As the countdown is started, the final decision is made whether the mission is a go. The mission can be scrubbed at any point in the process before the countdown clock reaches zero.

The countdown climaxes and the shuttle's engines ignite, burning 1,000 gallons of fuel every second. Within nine minutes, it has reached orbit. We will refer to this as the *Discovery Stage*. It is probably the most physically and mentally demanding stage for the astronauts as they catapult into space. This is where the astronauts discover what space flight really is about; simulators are nothing compared to the real thing. The launch is also very demanding on the shuttle and through it, we discover if the orbiter is capable of the task.

Once the shuttle reaches orbit, it positions itself into the right altitude to avoid earth's atmosphere. Once there, it is in the position to carry out its mission. We will refer to this as the *Deployment Stage*, where the shuttle has reached the intended place and the crew begins their work. As part of its assignment, the shuttle crew often will conduct numerous experiments. These experiments have resulted in many great contributions to mankind: from vascular pumps for heart patients to protective clothing for people with ultra sensitive skin, heat protection for stock cars, and even an advanced golf club.[4]

In addition to these experiments, the shuttle usually has a "main" task, which is the compelling reason for the mission. It is through the accomplishment of this task that the shuttle makes its greatest impact and fulfills its mission's design. The execution of its primary purpose is what we will call the *Destiny Stage*. All of the preparations, briefings, simulations, and hours of study have led to this period.

Now, let's see how these shuttle stages can help us understand life's journey. Like a shuttle mission, the journey to our *maxpoint* begins with the Decision Stage. This is not the decision to become a Christian, but rather the process of deciding what kind of a Christian you will become now that you are one. In other words, it is the process of deciding whether you will make the journey to your *maxpoint*. Will you decide that it is an important journey? Is the mission clear to you? Will you accept it? Will you do what is necessary to prepare for the launch and move through its various stages?

The keys that unlock the doors leading into the Decision Stage and the Discovery Stage are both found in Philippians 2:12-13, which says, "Therefore, my dear friends, as you have always obeyed — not only in my presence, but now much more in my absence — continue to work out your salvation with fear and trembling, for it is God who works in you to will and to act according to his good purpose."

---

[4] Source: http://spaceflight.nasa.gov/shuttle/benefits/index.html.

The first key is the phrase "to will." Before we can fully understand how this key operates, we need to grasp what Paul is telling the Philippian church. He instructs them to work *out* their salvation. Notice that Paul does not say they are to work *for* their salvation. He makes it clear in Ephesians 2:8-9 that we cannot work for our salvation; that is something that comes by grace and faith alone. Now that we have been saved from our sin, God expects us to work out that salvation. In other words, we need to "carry it to its full perfection."[5] We must follow through on what God has started in our lives.

Ephesians 2:10 explains that we are created "unto good works." Once we come to Christ, we are then truly capable of works that are good. Before Christ, even our best efforts are despicable to God. Paul reminds the Philippians that even though he is not there with them to monitor their spiritual growth, they still must give attention to it. The Philippians started the journey to their *maxpoint*, and they needed to give thought to reaching it. This is an important matter, one that Paul says they should approach with "fear and trembling."

Personal spiritual development is something to take seriously, and it is not something that happens by accident. You have to work at it. When you really think about it, everything else in life is linked to how well you "work out your salvation." Success in relationships, managing times of crisis, and good decision making are

---

[5] Jamieson, R., Fausset, A.R. & Brown, D. *Commentary Critical and Explanatory on the Whole Bible* (1871). Retrieved November 30, 2005, from www.bible.crosswalk.com.

determined by your walk with Christ. Trouble with your walk will affect these areas and more. The good news, however, is that we do not have to work out our salvation by ourselves. God does not just save us and then let us fend for ourselves. He saves us and continues to work actively in our lives, "for it is God who works in you to will and to act according to his good purpose."

This brings us to the ultimate question: what is life really about, anyway? It is much easier for us to progress in our salvation when we understand why Christ saved us in the first place. In the first chapter of Philippians, Paul answers that question when he writes in verses 20 and 21, "I eagerly expect and hope that I will in no way be ashamed, but will have sufficient courage so that now as always Christ will be exalted in my body, whether by life or by death. For to me to live is Christ and to die is gain." The word "exalted" means to magnify or to make great.[6] What was Paul saying? He was saying that the purpose of his life, even the purpose of his death, is to make great the Lord Jesus Christ.

Every situation Paul found himself in was an opportunity to exalt Christ. In a prison cell, Paul worshiped and magnified Christ. After being stoned and left for dead, Paul continued his ministry that Christ would be made great. Eventually, before Caesar and the highest officials of the Roman Empire, Paul would exalt the name of Jesus.

---

[6] Unger M. F., Vines, W.E. & White Jr., W. *Complete Expository Dictionary of Old and New Testament Words* (1985). Nashville: Thomas Nelson, page 386.

This is our purpose. This is why Christ saved us. If His purpose was simply to have us in Heaven with Him, He would have taken us there the moment we became saved. No, He leaves us here so we can reveal Christ to others. When things are going good in our life, it is so we can make Christ great. When things seem to be going badly, it likewise is to reveal Jesus. Why do bad things happen to good people? So good people can make Christ's name great.

Here is where that first key comes into use. "To will" means to align our will with God's will. It is the decision and commitment to seek to fulfill God's pleasure as the highest aim of our life. We are to will "according to His good purpose." That phrase also could be translated to "according to His pleasure" or "according to His good thoughts." At first glance, it would seem that what brings God pleasure and what brings us pleasure are mutually exclusive. And many times they are exclusive—but they don't have to be. I submit to you that ultimate pleasure in this life can only come by having our concept of pleasure meshed with God's concept.

Christ explained that real life comes by losing our life to God. "Then he said to them all: 'If anyone would come after me, he must deny himself and take up his cross daily and follow me. For whoever wants to save his life will lose it, but whoever loses his life for me will save it." (Luke 9:23-24). The psalmist tells us, "Delight yourself in the Lord and he will give you the desires of your heart" (Psalm 37:4). Our will aligns with God's as we daily consider ourselves dead and shift the focus of our affections to "things above, where Christ is seated at the right hand of God" (Col. 3:1).

Our view of God is a good starting place in determining where our affections are placed. Bob Sjogren, president of UnveilinGLORY Ministry, says that Christians have either a "cat" or a "dog" theology. He explains that you pet the cat, feed the cat, and talk to the cat. The cat says "hey, they pet me, feed me and care for me. I must be god. It is all about me." A dog, on the other hand, reacts differently. You pet, feed, and play with him and he says, "Wow! They do all that? They must be god. It is all about them." We approach God the same way. Cat Christians see the things that God has done and conclude that life is all about them — their comfort, their agenda, their praise. Dog Christians see the things that God has done and conclude that life is all about Him. They see His glory and desire to reflect it.

What does it take to awaken Christians to the fact that life is not all about them? How do we go from aimless wanderers to focused journeymen? What prompts us to align our will with God's? Many times it takes either a tragic act or an act of extreme faith. It is unfortunate, but it often takes a devastating accident or tragic life event to cause people to turn their focus to the Lord. But it doesn't have to be this way. It also could happen by the person taking a real step of faith — a step that requires total dependence upon God. It is a step off the edge of the known into the world of the unknown, with nothing but God as your safety net.

Some of the most effective tools I have ever seen to enable people to take this step are cross-cultural mission trips. The most effective kinds of trips are those that take you completely out of your comfort zone and connect you with the strategic movement of God. The more you move away from your routine and the things that are comfortable for you, the more God stretches and teaches you.

The Decision Stage, then, is all about aligning ourselves with God's will. It is embracing our purpose to make Christ known. It is allowing God to empower us to change course, if necessary, and place our life on a trajectory for our *maxpoint*. In a word, the Decision Stage is about *focus*: focus off us and on God.

Will is important and without it nothing can occur, but will alone is not enough. Will is meaningless unless it is accompanied by action, which brings us to the *Discovery Stage* of our journey. The key here is the phrase from Philippians 2:13 "to act." In the Decision Stage, we made the commitment to work out our salvation. In the Discovery Stage, we actually do it. In the Decision Stage, we shifted our focus from ourselves to God. In the Discovery Stage, we actually do the will of God. The single-word summary for the Discovery Stage is *obedience*.

Let's face it: obedience is not appealing. It isn't something we naturally gravitate toward. In fact, just the opposite is true. We don't like someone else telling us what to do. We want to be in control. We want to set our own course. We want independence. That is the problem: God expects the opposite. He requires us to be dependent—dependent on Him.

When the space shuttle moves through its ascent, it actually is totally dependent upon Mission Control and the automatic processes that NASA has put into place. The astronaut's job is to hold on and do exactly what Mission Control says. Why is this? Simple: Mission Control sees more than the astronauts can see. There are 50 people working the Control Room. They have the ability to monitor far more computers and instruments than the crew. Plus, they are the ones who planned and organized the mission, so they know it intimately.[7] The shuttle crew does not need to know all the information that Mission Control does. It would be overwhelming and too much to process. It would keep crew members from successfully accomplishing the immediate task before them.

God is our Mission Control. He sees things that we are not capable of seeing, including the future. He not only planned and organized our mission; He is the One who engineered us! It is silly for us not to let Mission Control take complete charge of our journey. He doesn't keep information from us simply for His enjoyment. He knows that if we knew everything going on around us and everything that will happen in the future, it would overwhelm us. We would be completely paralyzed. He shields us from certain information because He loves us.

This concept came to a new light for me after seeing the movie *The Passion of the Christ*. The movie, which chronicled the final 12 hours of Christ's life, showed flashbacks to earlier moments in his life. Many of these scenes were of Christ giving instruction to his disciples in light of the gruesome death that was to come. I began to marvel at the fact that Christ could function normally for

---

[7] Source: http://www.nasa.gov/audience/forstudents/9-12/ features/F_Mission_Control_Gets_Us_Into_Space.html.

33 years. If I knew about my death like Jesus knew about His, I probably would never have left the house. Christ fully knew the extensive suffering that He would endure. When Satan tempted him in the wilderness to abandon the "cross plan," He went forward with it anyway. Christ could handle that kind of knowledge. We cannot. It makes perfect sense for us to trust the All-seeing, All-knowing One and move forward with obedience.

The Discovery Stage is where our faith really develops. It is the season where we mature and gain the skills necessary to accomplish our ultimate mission. It is the time when we learn the daily disciplines that are vital to long-term success. It is where we get to practice obedience to both God's general will, which He expects of all believers, and His specific will, which pertains particularly to you. His general will is like First Stage Ascent. We must move through it before we can see the second stage. We must be faithful to what we know from Scripture that God expects of us before we can expect Him to reveal His specific will for us. The ascent to orbit only takes the shuttle about nine minutes; for us, it usually takes years. We will see this truth later as we examine the journeys of various biblical characters. What is important to note now is that there is no possible way to get to orbit without this stage. They may be able to do it in *Star Trek*, but in real life, you can't beam yourself into space. Likewise, there is no possible way to get to the place where your life is making a lasting, positive impact for Christ without learning obedience in the Discovery Stage.

It is sad that many Christians, maybe even a majority, never make it past the Discovery Stage. They abort the

journey and land with an ocean between themselves and where God wants them. Others will return to the launch site where they can slip into a previous comfort zone.

Then there are those who get stuck in the Discovery Stage. They stay stuck in a sub-par holding pattern. Maybe they stay in this pattern because they have found a new comfort zone to settle into. Perhaps it is because of a besetting sin. Possibly it is because they lack the drive or the faith to thrust into the next stage. Or they simply may have lost their first love and are not as passionate about Christ as they once were. Whatever the reason, it is tragic that these believers have come so far only to settle for less than their full potential. Now these are good people. They are faithful people. They are often obedient to the general will of God and to much of His specific will. They have grown much in the Lord, but now they have plateaued.

For those who break though the Discovery Stage, there is a breathtaking scene awaiting them. They look out the window and see things from a perspective few others ever will. This is fun! This is incredible! This is the Deployment Stage. The years of preparation, the daily discipline, the lifestyle of obedience are all worth it. The ascent was an incredible rush, but there is nothing like being in orbit. You are now in the place where you can really make an impact. The work of your hands is a blessing to many.

The Deployment Stage answers the question "Where do I fit?" It is about finding the best place to serve the Lord. It is not about what is good, but what is best. You see, God has a special place of service for you. Ephesians 2:10 says "For we are God's workmanship, created in Christ Jesus to do good works, which God prepared in advance for us to do." The word "workmanship" could also mean "work of art." God is trying to mold you into a masterpiece and that involves finding and doing the special work that God has for you. Jesus said in John 9:4, "As long as it is day, we must do the work of him who sent me. Night is coming, when no one can work." We have a limited amount of time to make as much of an impact for Christ as possible. We must find what God wants us to do and do it with all of our might. Paul tells us in Ephesians 4:12-13 that God gave us pastors and other ministry leaders, "To prepare God's people for works of service, so that the body of Christ may be built up until we all reach unity in the faith and in the knowledge of the Son of God and become mature, attaining to the whole measure of the fullness of Christ." You have a place to serve, but how can you know where is best for you?

Let me suggest that the most effective way for you to deploy for God is by aligning four "Ts": Task, Tale, Team, and Tools. *Task* is the particular job or ministry that you do. When you look at a ministry assignment, what actually will you do? *Tale* refers to your life message. What is the message that seems to resonate from your life? When you teach, talk to others, or just live each day, what is the sentence or phrase that best summarizes what you communicate? For example, if you had the same pastor for several years, you will pick up on a recurring theme in his messages. For my pastor, it would be the phrase "becoming a fully devoted follower of Christ." Billy Graham's tale would be "you must be born again." James Dobson's is "family first." Think about your pastor, as well as other pastors or speakers with whom you are familiar.

What would you say is their tale? Now, ask yourself what your tale is. If you don't know, ask a couple of people who have known you for a while.

Team refers to those with whom you will serve. What are they like? What are their strengths and weaknesses? What kind of personalities do they have? What is their passion? How will your strengths and skills complement the team? Is this a team that you want to be on? *Tools* are a collection of items acquired as you go through life. These include knowledge and abilities (born with and/or developed over time); spiritual gifts (given to you at the point of salvation); and experiences (good, bad or indifferent).

I have counseled numerous individuals considering career or ministry changes. When I was a mission agency executive, I conducted extensive interviews with people considering vocational missions. I also coached people as they came into our organization. What I found in these situations, as well as in my own life, is that when our task, tale, team, and tools are in harmony, we are most productive and happy. Find your place and deploy yourself for God's glory! The key word for the Deployment Stage is *impact*. You begin to make a significant impact with your life for the Lord.

The Deployment Stage is exciting, but there is still more. After a period of time, as you faithfully complete your projects and continue your personal development, you are ready to move into the *Destiny Stage*.

The Destiny Stage is the climax of the mission. For space shuttle crew members, this is when they will accomplish their greatest work. For us, this is where we reach our *maxpoint*, when we are fully utilized and are making the biggest impact possible for God's glory. We are operating at our fullest potential.

The Destiny Stage answers the question, "What is my legacy?" It also answers the question, "How is the world different because I lived?" The key word or focus of this stage is *multiplication*. It is about multiplying the impact of your godly influence through as many people as possible. It is making a difference in the lives of others that continues long after you are gone. It was said of Israel's King David, "For when David had served God's purposes in his own generation, he fell asleep; he was buried with his fathers ..." (Acts 13:36). David had a God-given destiny to accomplish, and he did it.

The Apostle Paul summarized his life this way, "For I am already being poured out like a drink offering, and the time has come for my departure. I have fought the good fight, I have finished the race, I have kept the faith. Now there is in store for me the crown of righteousness, which the Lord, the righteous Judge, will award to me on that day—and not only to me, but also to all who have longed for his appearing" (2 Timothy 4:6-8). Without regret, Paul looked back over the years since he became a Christian. His journey had been a marvelous one. He reached and sustained his *maxpoint*. He accomplished his God-appointed task. Now God had given him the grace and peace to die. He was ready to be delivered from the toil and challenges of this life. He was ready to be welcomed home.

When the time for our departure comes, will we be able to echo the words of Paul? Will we be able to look back on our life without any regrets? Will it be mission accomplished?

Ministry across the *Maxpoint* Stages

DECISION	DISCOVERY	DEPLOYMENT	DESTINY
focus	*obedience*	*impact*	*Multiplication*
Sporadic	─────────────────────▶		Continuous
Broad/ fragmented	─────────────────────▶		Specific, focused, unified
Unnatural	─────────────────────▶		Natural, second nature
Shallow	─────────────────────▶		Deep
Minimal impact	─────────────────────▶		Significant impact
Needs high supervision	─────────────────────▶		Supervisor
Low skill	─────────────────────▶		Highly skilled
Low commitment	─────────────────────▶		High commitment

Think about it ...

Which of the four *maxpoint* stages are you in right now?

Do you feel as if you are stuck in a stage? If so, for how long? Why?

How much does your will and God's will align?

Do you act like a cat or a dog?

Chapter 3
From Acorns to Oak Trees:
Fulfilling Our Destiny

One day my daughter, who was six at the time, came into the house and said, "Daddy, did you know that we have an oak tree in our front yard?" I responded, "No, that's not an oak tree," thinking the small tree I saw could not possibly be an oak.

"Yes, we have an oak tree in our front yard and I can prove it," Amber replied as she showed me a little acorn. To my surprise, she was right. Obviously, I am no horticulturalist! But I know that, given the right conditions, that little tree eventually will grow into a mighty one.

This is exactly what God wants to happen to us. As we journey to our *maxpoint*, God grows us into something beautiful, just like the oak tree. In the last chapter, we saw that God was actively working in our lives, empowering us to will and to act in accordance to His pleasure. We examined the various stages that God has laid out for us. Now, let's step back, observe the entire mosaic, and see what God has in store for us. Let's discover the fascinating principles of the acorn.

Mike Jorgensen of GoLeaders.net says that an acorn is like a bomb: not potentially explosive but full of explosive potential. He likens believers to acorns with this explosive potential. For example, in a good year, a healthy white oak tree can produce as many as 2,300 acorns. With a 90 percent survival rate, that's about 2,070 saplings. One acorn can eventually turn into 2,070 trees. That little acorn has the potential to reseed an entire forest!

There are two acorn principles that apply to us. The first is that, like the acorn, God has placed within us everything necessary to explode into a forest of fruitfulness for Him. The second is that to be successful, all we have to do is what we are designed to do. The acorn principle is found in Isaiah 61:1-3, which prophetically speaks of Christ.

> *"The Spirit of the Sovereign LORD is on me, because the LORD has anointed me to preach good news to the poor. He has sent me to bind up the brokenhearted, to proclaim freedom for the captives and release from darkness for the prisoners, to proclaim the year of the LORD's favor and the day of vengeance of our God, to comfort all who mourn, and provide for those who grieve in Zion — to bestow on them a crown of beauty instead of ashes, the oil of gladness instead of mourning, and a garment of praise instead of a spirit of despair. They will be called oaks of righteousness, a planting of the LORD for the display of his splendor."*

God desires to take us like acorns and turn us into mighty trees of righteousness, all for His glory. Everything you and I need for this to be accomplished is given through Jesus Christ. Think about what Jesus Christ did, and as our perfect example, what we also should do. The passage says, "*The Spirit ... is on me because the LORD has anointed me to preach good news ...*" Jesus Christ came to proclaim good news. Christ left the riches, the wonder, the splendor, and the glory of Heaven to walk along dusty roads, to be nailed to a cross, and suffer the most excruciating death known to the world at that time, in order to pay for our sins. This truly is good news! The fact that our sins could be forgiven and that we can have a home in Heaven is something to shout about. Yes, Jesus brought good news.

Don't you love to hear good news? Don't you love to be the bearer of good news? We have the opportunity today to do just that as we share with others the message of Christ. We have the privilege of taking that good news into the streets of our Jerusalem, Judea, Samaria, and even to the very ends of the earth. The good news is that Jesus Christ came that we might have life and that we might have it more abundantly.

Becoming all that God would have us to become is tied to our sharing this good news with others. A vital part of our mission is to help others become followers of Christ. It is living our life as a lighthouse that guides others to the safe harbor of Jesus. It is taking advantage of opportunities to herald salvation's good news to others. We are left here on earth to spread the gospel as we make our journey. For those of us who have been saved for a long time and live in nations with high numbers of "professing Christians," we may assume that the good news is actually old news. *Surely people have heard about Christ and are at least somewhat familiar with the gospel*, we may mistakenly think. This could not be further from the truth. The fact is that the

United States, England, and other nations once considered "Christian" have become so pluralistic and secular that they actually are post-Christian. With each generation, there is less emphasis on spiritual matters, so multitudes now have little or no exposure to church and even less understanding of the Bible.

I was walking through a shopping mall one day when a 20-something-year-old man selling cell phones stopped me. I was moving past his kiosk with no intention of stopping, when he commented about the shirt I was wearing with the name of my college alma mater on it. "I've never heard of that university," he said, obviously trying to strike up a conversation that would turn into a phone sale. "Where is it?" I told him that it was a Christian university. "Oh, they would never have me then," he replied, "I'm not a Christian."

He began to share with me that it wasn't that he was opposed to Christianity; he just didn't really know much about it. "I know there is a God, and that there is probably more to life than what I am experiencing, but I don't know what that is." He explained that he had never gone to church. His parents were not "religious," and church was never on his family's radar screen. He knew he had sinned and felt guilt about the things he had done, but didn't know what could be done about it.

I shared with him the good news of Christ and the forgiveness He offered. I explained to him the difference between having "religion" and having a relationship with God. No one had ever taken the time to explain these truths to him, even though one of his co-workers professed to be a Christian. He didn't accept Christ that day, but he did hear the good news. "You have really given me something to think about," he said as we parted paths. "Thank you." This man is typical of many who have had no legitimate exposure to the gospel.

Notice in the passage that Christ says He came to "*bind up the broken-hearted.*" Jesus Christ came not only to preach, but to heal. When we think about healing, we often think about the terrible diseases like cancer that can ravage our bodies. Jesus certainly heals these diseases as He chooses. But there is a disease much greater than cancer or Parkinson's or anything known to modern medicine. It is the disease of sin. No doctor can cure this disease. No medicine can dissolve it. It is a disease that only the Great Physician can heal.

That's why Jesus Christ came. He came so that we could be healed. He came so that you and I could take that healing to the nations, so that others could be saved. As the great spiritual cardiologist, Christ magnificently restores hearts broken by the ravages of sin. There are many people today whose spirit, life, and heart have been crushed by the sins of others. They have been so badly hurt emotionally that healing does not seem possible. Yet, even in the direst of situations, Christ is able to restore what was broken and make it more complete. Sometimes their hearts are crushed by their own sin. The guilt resulting from poor decisions, hurtful actions toward others or self-destructive behavior gnaws at them. Christ brings complete healing to these situations as well.

Christ came not only to heal the disease of sin, but also to deliver us from its bondage. The passage says that Christ came to "*proclaim freedom for the captives, and release from darkness for the prisoners."* There are so many people today who are in bondage to sin. Even Christians, those who tasted freedom, have walked right back into the prison cell. We have been pardoned, our crime has been paid in full by Christ, yet how often do we put on sin's handcuffs—all when there are multitudes of people who have never tasted the freedom of forgiveness?

I witnessed a stunning example of sin's bondage while ministering in the Russian city of Orsk. Located about 900 miles southeast of Moscow, this city of about 350,000 people was an epicenter of drug and alcohol abuse. Although the sun shone while we were there, darkness prevailed.

My interpreter and I, along with a member from an area church, visited a lady who was an alcoholic. Her husband had an affair, left her, and somehow ended up in prison. She had contemplated suicide many times and told me that she would have done it if it hadn't been for her nine-year-old daughter. She told me of her struggles, her search for significance and meaning, and how out of control her life was. She had tried various religions, even dabbled in the occult.

I shared Christ with her and challenged her to make a decision. "It is not Jesus Christ plus your sin," I told her. "You have to turn away from your sin and trust Jesus alone for your salvation." After a long pause, she replied, "I know I cannot be on the fence. I know I cannot serve God and the devil, but I'm just not ready to serve God." She was in prison but would not accept the pardon. Although her story was repeated in the lives of many others in Orsk, we did see some glimmers of hope.

One of our witnessing teams went into an apartment building to visit a family. It is the custom to take off your shoes when entering a Russian home. But this time, our team members were instructed not to remove their shoes. They soon noticed why. There were needles and drug paraphernalia everywhere. This apartment building was home to many hard-core drug addicts.

In spite of the surroundings, our team of "ordinary" American church members began sharing Christ with the residents. They told these troubled men and women about Jesus and how He could unlock the door of sin that held them captive. Several people responded positively to the gospel. They made the decision to turn away from their sin and embrace Christ. The team returned several times over the next few days to conduct follow-up Bible study lessons. Each time, the former "captives" invited their imprisoned friends from other apartments so that they too could discover the key to unlock their cell of sin. They learned firsthand that Christ indeed sets the captives free.

One of the most beautiful phrases in Scripture is found in this Isaiah passage. It tells how Christ would "bestow on them a crown of beauty instead of ashes ... garments of praise instead of a spirit of despair." Old Testament Jews who were in mourning would spread ashes across their face and head and then dress in sackcloth. The beautiful picture God gives here is Christ washing away the dirty ashes and placing on the person a beautiful crown. The person throws off his garment of despair and replaces it with the beautiful threads of praise.

Mark, a former fireman from Ohio, saw this verse come to life right before his eyes. Mark was part of a team witnessing in a small Romanian town. He was waiting for a ride to join the rest of his team when he noticed a young woman at the nearby bus stop with a baby in her arms. Her brightly colored dress, like her body, was dirty. She was isolated from some other women who also were waiting for a bus. It was obvious that they were keeping their distance from the young mother, who was Roma. The Roma people, better known by their slang name "Gypsy," are considered by many to be the outcasts of society. They are looked upon with distrust and apprehension. Mark saw her and said to himself, *I need to share Jesus with her.*

He told her God loves her. As he spoke, she began to cry. She couldn't believe that anyone outside of her ethnic group would speak to her, let alone someone all the way from America. Mark shared the gospel with her, and at that bus stop, she opened her life to Jesus Christ. After that, Mark and the young woman went their separate ways, both figuring they would never see each other again this side of Heaven.

A year later, Mark was back in Romania, this time ministering in a small city a few miles away from where he had been the previous year. He was standing on a sidewalk, witnessing to a group of people, when he noticed a beautiful, nicely dressed woman who began to approach the crowd. She walked with poise and confidence. As she got closer, Mark realized this was the same filthy, ragged, depressed-looking woman he had led to Christ the year before. Everything about her had changed.

She told Mark what happened after the bus-stop encounter. "I went home that day and told my family what happened. I told them how you came and shared the love of Jesus with me and how I invited Christ into my life. Christ changed my life that day and I have been living for Him ever since. But my family did not understand, especially my brother. He said, 'You're crazy, crazy! To be a Christian, it's crazy.'"

For a year, she lived this out before her family members. They saw how Christ had bestowed on her a crown of beauty instead of the ashes of despair. Now, a few feet away from Mark, another group gathered, listening to the gospel. Among them was this woman's brother, and this became his day of salvation! He told one of our team members, "A year ago my sister came home and told me about Jesus. I told her that she was crazy. Do you know what? Well, I must be crazy now too."

That is beauty from ashes. God took someone the world said was worthless and should be cast aside, and He invaded her life with peace, joy, and purpose. That's what God does. And that is what God does when He moves in His acorns to produce beautiful oak trees.

You see, all we need to do is what God created us to do. What is that, you may ask? Why are you alive today? One reason: *His glory*. That's why you were created. You were created for God's glory. That's why that Gypsy woman was created. She was created for God's glory. Every person walking on the face of this earth was created for God's glory. Our text says that He wants to make us an oak of righteousness, a splendid plant of His.

I remember a childhood vacation where we saw the giant redwoods and sequoia trees of California. These trees were so huge that a hole had been cut through one wide enough to drive a car through. What splendor! That is exactly what God wants to do with us. He wants to make us an incredible display of His splendor and glory so that we point many people toward Him. Those magnificent trees pointed all who gazed at them to Heaven. Likewise, as you maximize your life for God's glory, you will point people toward Heaven.

Mark, the former fireman and paramedic who led the Gypsy woman to Christ, is a good example of this. One icy winter day in Ohio, Mark was participating in a fire training exercise when his life drastically changed. He had his full gear on—including the breathing apparatus—as he stretched a hose line from the fire truck across a parking lot. As he moved across the lot in a blizzard, he slipped on the ice like one would slip on a banana and injured his back. He went through three months of rehabilitation before returning to work for eight months. Later he re-injured his back and was sent to the hospital.

This time, the doctors said a fire career no longer would be possible. Both Mark and his wife, who is a nurse, were devastated. "It was like losing a family member," Mark said. He went back on light duty to finish his time. Confined to a desk, it was torture every time a call came in, but he could not respond with his unit. "Like telling a fish not to swim or a bird not to sing is how I felt each time there was a call. You want to respond, but you're hit in the face with the reality that you can't."

Several months later, with Mark feeling worthless and without direction now that life as he knew it was gone, his wife heard about a short-term mission trip to Romania. "You should do this," she told Mark. Well, Mark did and that decision changed his life. In Romania, he saw the incredible ways that God could use him. He discovered that life was more than a career—it was about serving the Giver of Life. The fire department no longer had a use for Mark, but that certainly didn't mean that God didn't. In fact, it was quite the opposite. Mark was now seeing himself through the eyes of God—which looked upon Mark with love, fondness, and the desire to use him in great ways. He was no longer a firefighter rescuing lives from momentary danger, but he was a tree pointing people to the Savior who could rescue them for eternity. Today, Mark is attending Bible college and preparing for vocational ministry. He also is extremely active in his church, assisting his pastor.

If we are a healthy tree, then we are going to produce fruit. Like Mark, this may come as a surprise to us. It may come as an even bigger surprise when we see the way God actually accomplishes this. I'm sure no one was as surprised about God's movement through his life as Charles from Arkansas, who went on a mission trip to Venezuela. There, he saw four rough-looking guys standing on a street corner and asked God to help him witness to them. All four of them ended up praying with Charles to receive Christ as their Savior. Unknown to Charles, one of those men happened to be the top "hit man" in the region. That night, the new creature in Christ was in church, instead of out working with drug dealers.

The same evening, in the same town, a Christian woman suddenly awoke. "I heard a voice that said 'get out of your bed,'" she later reported. "This never happened before, but I heard a voice say, 'get up and get out of bed.'"

So, in the middle of the night, she got up and went to another room. Seconds later, she heard a gunshot in her bedroom. She went back in, and to her shock, saw that a bullet had been fired into the room—into the very pillow on which she had been sleeping. The next night, she brought the bullet to church and shared the incredible story of how God had protected her.

The hit-man-turned-Christian was also at that service. He began to compare stories with the woman and they figured out what happened. Some men tried to hire this hit man to kill someone, but they couldn't find him because he was in church. So, they hired the number-two "hit man" in town for the job, but he mistakenly went to the wrong house—the house of the woman. God spared two lives that night, and who knows how many more now that this "hit man" has left his profession.

Just think, God used one of his oak trees named Charles to get on an airplane, go to a country he had never been to before, travel into a city whose name he couldn't pronounce, and utilize an interpreter he had never met before to talk to some tough guys about Christ—probably with his knees knocking the whole time he was doing it. Now there is a former "hit man" who worships God. Pretty amazing, isn't it? It is amazing what God can do with each of us.

Think about it ...

Are you in any kind of spiritual bondage right now? If so, what should you do about it?

How are you sharing Christ's good news?

Does your life resemble an oak tree or does it look more like an acorn?

Chapter 4
Discover What?

Earlier we noticed there is a critical stage God must take us through to become that incredible oak of righteousness. We called it the Discovery Stage. But what specifically does God want us to discover? What must we master before we can move into the Deployment Stage? While there are many, many things that we should be learning and becoming as Christians, there are some core components that Christ expects of us. I would imagine that coming to Christ as an adult would almost be overwhelming. There is so much about God to learn. There is so much about ourselves that we need to learn now that we are new creations. Where do we start? I would propose that we start with Christ and His outline for becoming a full-fledged disciple.

Jesus tells us in the Great Commission of Matthew 28:18-20 that we are to make disciples by reaching people, baptizing them, and "teaching them to observe whatever I have commanded you." The method of disciple making, or mastering the Discovery Stage, is found in that last phrase. It is by learning to observe the things that Christ specifically commanded. Now there are many things that Jesus taught. They are all important for us to know and apply, but we can begin with His specific commands. A study of these direct commands of Christ in the Gospels and Acts will reveal nine areas for us to master. They are salvation, evangelism, missions, relationships, heart issues, daily living, spiritual victory, vigilance, and persecution.

We begin with the foundation of all things, which is salvation from sin and the reception of everlasting life. Let's face it: the concept of salvation through faith in Christ is the complete opposite of our post-modern, post-Christian world. Christians are often accused of being "narrow-minded" because we believe in universal truth (objective standards that do not change over time and apply to all people), while society teaches individual truth (that which is relevant to me or what I consider to be true). The fact is we are narrow-minded — that is the nature of truth. Truth excludes falsehoods. Jesus made it perfectly clear that the way to salvation is a narrow way (Matthew 7:13-14; Luke 13:22-24). Jesus illustrates it as a narrow gate that one must go through intentionally. Although available to all people, most will not accept salvation because of its exclusiveness. True salvation from our sin excludes religion or "self-works" as a means to attain it. Salvation is only through a relationship with God the Father through the Son Jesus Christ.

Jesus' message from the very beginning of his public ministry was "repent and believe" (Mark 1:15). Salvation is a two-sided coin, with repentance on one side and faith on the other. We turn away from our sin and we turn to Christ, believing that His death, burial and resurrection are all that is necessary to secure forgiveness. This is the starting place for the journey to our *maxpoint*. Without it, we are headed down a broad road that leads to destruction. The Scriptures exhort us to make sure we have this issue settled. If you doubt whether you are truly a born-again child of God who has been made into a new creation, you cannot progress in any meaningful way in your spiritual journey. The issue of salvation must be settled.

The second area that we need to grasp is that of evangelism: sharing the gospel message with those who do not know it, with the prayer that they will accept it for themselves. Jesus told a group of professional fishermen that if they would follow Him, He would make them spiritual fishermen. He would enable them to reach people for Himself (Mark 1:16-18). God has us in this world as His ambassadors, to be His mouthpieces, to deliver His message of forgiveness and salvation to the masses of humanity. God doesn't send angels to proclaim the gospel because they have not and cannot experience salvation. No, God sends His children, those adopted into His family and who know what it means to pass from spiritual death into life. Fishing for people should be as much a priority and urgency as a fisherman fishing for his life's sustenance. It should be something we do with intention.

Sadly, the topic of evangelism strikes fear in the hearts of many believers. "What do I say?" "What if they ask me a question I don't know how to answer?" "What if they reject me?" These and many more questions float through our minds when the topic of evangelism is raised. We must, however, keep in mind that God calls us to be witnesses ... to share with others what we have seen and experienced. One of the most powerful witnessing tools is our own testimony of how we came to faith in Christ. What was our life like before Christ? What were the factors that led to our decision to commit our lives to Christ? How did we come to grasp the death, burial, and resurrection of Christ as full payment for our sins? What have our lives been like since receiving the Lord? Discovering how to witness effectively is a core competency that must be mastered before we can move from the Discovery to the Deployment Stage.

"Missions" is simply the "going" of evangelism. It is taking the message of Christ to the people. Think of it this way: missions is going, and evangelism is what you do when you get there. The going may be across the street, across the country, across cultures or across the world. It is going with a purpose: to reach and disciple people for Christ. Missions is not a program, project or proposal. Christ intended it to be a lifestyle — and not just for a select few, but for all believers. That lifestyle has two expressions: sending and going. It is doing what we can to send people into God's harvest fields through our prayers (Luke 10:2; Matthew 9:38) and our finances (Philippians 4:15-19).

While the "passive" activities of praying and giving are critical, they do not relinquish our call to be active in going to the lost with the gospel. That activity should be in our Jerusalem (local area), but it also should be to the ends of the earth (Acts 1:8). Jesus *never* taught that we should reach all of our Jerusalem *before* reaching out to the ends of the earth. A careful study of the Acts passage reveals that God intends for us to reach out to our Jerusalem *while* we are also reaching out to the ends of the earth. In fact, my experience has been that churches with dynamic "passive" and "active" ends of the earth endeavors have, as a byproduct, a dynamic Jerusalem ministry. When you see firsthand how God can use you cross-culturally to make an impact, you realize how He can use you at home in your own culture. When you act with compassion and concern for the lost in distant lands, it naturally raises your awareness of the lost at home.

Another core competency that we must acquire in the Discovery Stage is how we relate to others. Jesus had much to say about relationships, and for good reason. Next to our relationship with God, our relationship with others is the most vital area to which we could give attention. Relationships are an incredible driving force in our lives, either positively or negatively. No one is an island to himself or herself. To be effective for Christ, to reach and maintain our *maxpoint*, we must learn how to get along with others. Those relationships that we must guard, according to Christ, include relationships with other Christians (Matthew 5:23-24, 6:12-15, 18:15-22 ff; Luke 17:3-4); our spouse (if we are married, Mark 10:2-9); children (Mark 10:13-16; Luke 18:16); enemies (Matthew 5:44); and simply people in general (Luke 6:37; John 7:24, 13:14, 15:17; Matthew 5:38, 22:39).

Christ commands us to live at peace with others (Mark 9:50). He also knew that some conflict in relationships was inevitable. As long as we are sinful and fallible, there are going to be damaged relationships. But Christ's desire is for relationships not to stay that way, but to be reconciled. In fact, being reconciled with others is more important than worshiping God (Matthew 5:23-26) because damaged relationships also damage our ability to worship God in sincerity and in truth. It does not matter whether we are the offending party or the one offended. If we are aware of a rift, it is our responsibility to lovingly seek reconciliation. God is also concerned about relationships within the Body of Christ that have been strained because of sin. Our call is to reach out, again in love, to those who have strayed so they may be restored (Galatians 6:1; Matthew 18:15-17).

The most important skill we can master when it comes to relationships is how to forgive and to seek forgiveness (Luke 17:1-4). Giving forgiveness, even if the other person has not asked for it, is a conscious decision on your part. It is not an act of emotion. Nor is it your best effort to push the offense out of your memory. It is the willful choice to no longer hold the offense against that person. Giving forgiveness means that once the choice is made, the offense cannot be brought up again. If my wife wrongs me and I grant her forgiveness, then I cannot use that incident as a "weapon" in future fights. I cannot remind her of what she did and try to use that to my advantage. If it is forgiven, it is dropped. That "sword" can never be picked up and used again.

It is also important to grasp what it means to seek forgiveness. It is not saying that you are *sorry* for something. My kids are sorry when I catch them in an act of disobedience. I am sorry if I make my wife cry or get angry. Proclaiming your sorrow is not the same as seeking forgiveness. Sorrow may be part of the process, but it is not the same as forgiveness. The steps to seeking forgiveness from others are the same as seeking forgiveness from God. First, there must be an admission of the wrong: "I was wrong to do …" Next, there must be an understanding of the hurt the action caused: "I know it hurt you." Then, there can be an acknowledgement of your feelings: "I am so sorry for what I have done." Finally, the request for forgiveness can come: "Will you forgive me?"

Forgiveness is a powerful force. I have seen this illustrated in an incredible way through the lives of my parents. Although both are Christians, my parents divorced when I was a young child. They each later remarried. When I was 12 years old, we had a revival team ministering at our church. They taught on the subject of seeking forgiveness for the things that you have done — even if others had also offended you. My mother took that to heart and decided that she needed to ask my dad for forgiveness. So, after the special revival service one night, we stopped to see my dad and stepmother. I waited in the car while my mom and stepfather went inside. With my step mom present, my mother asked forgiveness of my dad for her shortcomings in their marriage. My dad responded by granting his forgiveness and by seeking my mom's forgiveness for what he had done wrong in the marriage. The two couples prayed together for some time, and then we left.

I must tell you that what happened since that night is nothing short of a miracle. Although restoring my parents' marriage was not an option, those acts of forgiveness did restore the relationship. That also created a great relationship between my mother and stepmother. In fact, some time after that night of forgiveness, my stepmother said to me, "You know, I don't think of your mom as your dad's ex-wife. I think of her as one of my sisters." We would go on to share Christmases and other special occasions together. Even after I moved across country, my dad and step mom would visit my mother's parents along with my mom and step dad. It truly is an amazing situation that was all brought about because of forgiveness.

In addition to our outward relationships, Jesus commands us to give attention to what is happening inside, in our heart. Proverbs 4:23 says, "Above all else, guard your heart, for it is the wellspring of life." Jesus echoed this principle when he said, "Be careful, or your hearts will be weighed down with dissipation, drunkenness, and the anxieties of life, and that day will close on you unexpectedly life a trap." For what particularly must we watch? Judging others (Luke 6:37; John 7:24; Matthew 7:1); lusting (Matthew 5:28); anger (Matthew 5:22); discontentment (John 6:43); worry (John 14:1; Luke 12:22; Matthew 6:25ff); fear (John 14:27, Luke 5:10, 12:7, 12:32); and not having proper or pure motives (Matthew 6:1-4) are all items that we must vigilantly keep out of our lives.

Now that we have looked inward, we need to look outward to see how we are adopting Christ's instructions as our daily actions. He says that we should be generous with our time and resources to care for others (Luke 12:33, 14:12-14, 6:38). We must guard against hypocrisy (Matthew 23:2-7); pay attention to what we say (Matthew 5:37); and act with humility (Luke 14:8). It is critical that we order our lives so it prioritizes the Lord (Luke 12:31-33; John 6:27; Matthew 6:19-21, 6:33, 19:21), which is demonstrated by how we use our time, talents, and treasures to put Him first in everything.

The Discovery Stage is about learning to love — to love God with all of our heart, soul, and mind (Matthew 22:37). It is about developing that love relationship with God. It is no surprise that Jesus had much to say about this, as He challenged us to stay in His love (John 15:9) by staying vitally connected to Him (John 15:4; Matthew 11:28), so we could love the Lord appropriately (Mark 12:29-31). Our relationship is strengthened as we seek holiness (Matthew 5:48); deny the flesh through fasting (Matthew 6:16-18); and remain vigilant in prayer (Matthew 6:9, 7:7-12, 26:41; Luke 22:40 & 46). Like any relationship, our relationship with Christ must be given attention. We must stay alert to Him and to challenges around us that could hinder our walk (Matthew 24:42, 25:1; Luke 12:35, 17:3; Mark 13:32-35), but we must not let those challenges keep us from stepping out in faith (Mark 11:22).

There are two final subjects that we must grasp in the Discovery Stage. The first is deception. While deception is a danger throughout our spiritual journey, it is especially worrisome in the early days of our Christian walk and in the beginning stages of the trajectory to our *maxpoint*. The cults prey on Christians who are not grounded in their faith. Satan especially charms those who are inexperienced in spiritual living and warfare. We must watch for deception (Mark 13:5; Matthew 24:4; Luke 21:8) and guard our hearts and minds from its influence (Matthew 16:5-6; Luke 12:1). Deception can come from false prophets (Matthew 7:15) and from those who may teach the Bible but do so in a distorted way (Luke 20:46; Mark 12:38; Matthew 7:15); from people who seem very religious (*the*

Pharisees, Mark 8:15) and from those who have political or societal power (*Herod,* Mark 8:15).

The last subject in our Discovery Stage is not a popular one with many of us, but it is one that Jesus addresses head on. That is the subject of persecution. Christ, in all of His teachings, never painted a rosy picture of what it would mean to follow Him. In fact, it was just the opposite. He made it clear that the life He was calling us to would not be an easy one, but it would be an abundantly rewarding one. Jesus in no uncertain terms told His followers that persecution was coming, and it would be a normal part of their existence (John 15:20; Mark 13:9, 13:11, 13:23).

I must admit that growing up in the United States, I have no real concept of what it means to be persecuted for my faith. I have met many people around the world who truly have been persecuted, but I don't have firsthand experience. My natural self says, *yes, and I don't ever want to learn firsthand what persecution mean!* I stand in amazement as I see those who do not run from persecution, but actually embrace it. As we will see in a later chapter, they, like the Apostle Paul, have learned the incredible benefits of persecution.

I was in Russia conducting leadership training for about 30 pastors and lay leaders. We started our two-day session with introductions: everyone shared their name and a little bit about their ministry. I was feeling great and excited about the materials I was going to teach until one older gentleman stood up to introduce himself. He shared how he had been a pastor under Communism. He told how, despite government orders, he boldly preached

Christ and sought to win the lost. Then he said it led to 15 years in a Siberian prison. I could only imagine what those years were like. I could only imagine the deplorable conditions he endured. *What do I have to say to these men,* I thought after this man shared his story. *What could I possibly teach that man?* Persecution has been part of the history of the church from its inception, and it will continue to be in many places. Whatever persecution might come our way, we must discover God's grace in it and boldly determine it will not make us bitter or cause us to be silent; but rather, we will see it as an opportunity to grow in our faith and witness.

There is much for us to learn in the Discovery Stage. It could seem overwhelming, but it doesn't have to be. The exhortation of that old gospel song "One day at a time, sweet Jesus" is a good one. The Discovery Stage is simply living one day at a time, as we faithfully learn the lessons that our Sweet Jesus has for us that particular day. Start and end your day with the Lord. In the middle, have a prayerful attitude that seeks to be aware of what God is doing in and around you. Then, in the fullness of time, God will move you to your *maxpoint*.

Think about it ...

Which of the nine discovery areas (salvation, evangelism, missions, relationships, heart issues, daily living, spiritual victory, vigilance, and persecution) is your weakest? How can you grow in this area?

Is there anyone you're holding a grudge against that you need to forgive?

Is there anyone whose forgiveness you need to seek?

Chapter 5
The Journey Illustrated

Biographies are extremely popular. There is even a cable television channel devoted exclusively to biographies. We love to learn about people, and we love to learn from them. Biographies are good because they can give us insights into ourselves. They allow us to learn from both the successes and mistakes of others. As we consider the journey to our *maxpoint*, it is helpful to glean insights from those who journeyed before us. Let's open the pages of a few biographies and see what we can discover.

We first return to Abraham's biography. When we last saw Abraham, he was just starting his journey in response to God's call to leave his comfort zones. One thing we learn early in Abraham's story is not to confuse the journey with our *maxpoint*. God called Abraham to go to a land that He would show him. God also promised to make him a great nation. Abraham obeyed and arrived in Canaan, but he was still far from his *maxpoint*. That would not come until many years later.

Something else we notice about Abraham's journey is that it was filled with detours. Unfortunately, Abraham succumbed to at least two of them. The first detour took him and his wife Sarah to Egypt to escape a local famine. Apparently, Sarah was quite beautiful, and Abraham was afraid the Egyptians would kill him to have her. So he lied and said that his wife was his sister. The lie eventually was discovered, and Abraham was deported. He returned to Canaan.

The second detour came much later, when Sarah presented Abraham a plan to "help God" after many years without the son of promise. "Listen, Abraham," she said, "maybe we're missing something. God said He would give us a child, right? Well, surely God must have meant it would be by my handmaid, Hagar, since I am not able to bear children. Why don't you have relations with her?" Abraham obliged and Hagar gave birth to Ishmael, but this was not the son of promise. Abraham took a detour — the detour of impatience. He didn't want to wait until God fulfilled his promise. Abraham tried the shortcut.

There is no shortcut around God's plan. God is working on us, and that takes time. We don't get to our *maxpoint* overnight. God works in our lives, introducing experiences that help mold, develop, and chip away our rough areas. Abraham tried to rush the process, but this simply doesn't work. This is a hard fact for many of us to grasp, since we live in an "instant" society. We want instant food and instant coffee, and we can't live without instant messages. With the click of the mouse, we can instantly send an electronic letter halfway around the world, and a few seconds later, receive a response. I can instantly talk to anyone, anywhere, by grabbing the cell phone clipped to my belt. Or if I prefer, I can send them an instant text message. I don't have to wait for the late news to see sports scores because they are already displayed on my pager as the game is progressing. We can expect technology to make other parts of our lives "instant," but we can never expect reaching our *maxpoint* to be instant. Some things just take time.

Abraham returned to his journey of faith. He got back on the road and began once again to trust God completely. It is interesting that even though Abraham was a wealthy man, he did not put his faith in his possessions. Genesis 14:14 tells us that Abraham had 318 servants *born* into his household. In other words, the people that were working for him gave birth to 318 children who became Abraham's warriors and workers. This means that Abraham was CEO of a mid-size corporation! He had 500 to 1,000 employees. Abraham was a wealthy man—*extremely* wealthy, but he did not trust in his wealth. We know this from the events of Genesis 14.

Following a successful military victory, Abraham was met by a priest of the Lord named Melchizedek. Melchizedek blessed Abraham who responded by giving 10 percent of everything he owned. This was *long* before Moses and the law called for a tithe. Abraham tithed because he wanted to tithe. Now it's one thing when you're a young child and you tithe on your dollar allowance. It is quite another when you are making "real money" and are called to give a portion. Abraham was not trusting in his own resources and found it easy to give what he had to Melchizedek.

The next thing we notice about Abraham's journey is that the *maxpoint* is not always obvious. At the age of 100, Abraham finally had the fulfillment of God's promise: Isaac was born. At first glance, it would seem that this was Abraham's *maxpoint*. After all, everything in his life had been building up to that moment. Abraham's *maxpoint*, however, was still to come. Isaac was the result of God's faithfulness. It wasn't so much about Abraham as it was about God. God said, "I'm going to do this, and I swear by myself that this will come to pass." God had unconditionally promised offspring to Abraham.

Abraham's *maxpoint* actually came several years after Isaac was born when God told Abraham to sacrifice his son on the mountains of Moriah. Without hesitation and without trying to argue with God, Abraham began the process. Abraham could do this because by this point, his faith in God was incredibly strong. Hebrews 11 tells us that Abraham was totally convinced that God was going to resurrect his son from the dead. He totally believed that he was going to kill his son and God was going to bring him back to life. No doubt about it. Instead, God stopped Abraham just moments before he was to kill his son. Abraham had reached his *maxpoint*. His incredible demonstration of faith has impacted generations, and it continues to impact us today. This was the place where God wanted Abraham to arrive. This was the place where he brought God maximum glory.

One final note about Abraham: not only did he impact future generations, but he had a powerful impact on those around him. In Genesis 24, we have the story of Abraham sending his chief of staff off to find a wife for his son Isaac. When he arrived near the designated city, he stopped at a well and began to pray. "O Lord, God of my master Abraham, give me success today ..." (verse 12). This is the first time in Scripture that God is identified with a man, "God of ... Abraham." How did this servant know to seek the Lord? How did he know that he could have confidence that God would guide him? He knew because Abraham had made God known.

God told Abraham what the result of his faithfulness would be, but He did not give Abraham details about the journey. God often does the same with us. He lays on our heart a calling or mission for our life, but does not give the details of what it will take to get there. The details are what we must work through by faith. We see a similar pattern in the life of Joseph.

When we first meet Joseph in Genesis 37, we are introduced to a 17-year-old who is loved dearly by his father but despised by his 11 brothers. It seems that Joseph was a bit of a tattletale, which, coupled with his father's favoritism, did not win him much support from the rest of the family. To make matters worse, Joseph had a dream about his family all bowing to him, which he naively announced to his clan.

As a teenager, God gave Joseph a vision for his life, but it wasn't very detailed. Joseph would one day be in a place of honor and authority, but he had no idea what it would take to get there. Over the next 13 years, he would be rejected by his family, traded as a slave, maligned, falsely imprisoned, and forgotten by those he helped. It was exactly as God planned.

Joseph had a vibrant relationship with the Lord, and God blessed him. As a servant in an Egyptian official's house, Joseph magnified God. His boss, Potiphar, saw God through Joseph. He could not help but notice that God was with Joseph. So Potiphar put Joseph in charge of everything he had, with no concern except for what he ate. As far as Joseph knew, there was no room for advancement. This was as high on the corporate ladder that he could climb. He believed he would be with Potiphar until the Egyptian died or grew tired of Joseph. Most of us would slack off in a "dead-end" situation like this. We would not give 100 percent of our effort. Not Joseph. He did not allow his seeming lack of a future to affect his work ethic—and that's good because God was using this assignment to teach Joseph some important management skills that would be critical later in life.

Things were improving for Joseph when suddenly, he was hit with a scandal. His boss's wife was accusing him of trying to seduce her. Even though it was actually the other way around, everyone believed her. Only God, Joseph, and the wife knew the truth—and she chose to lie about it. It was a tough situation to be in, having your reputation tarnished and your character assassinated. Things quickly turned from bad to worse, and Joseph was sent to prison. No trial. No appeals process. Prison it was. Joseph simply tried to do what was right. It seemed he was paying the price for his good morals—or was he?

At first glance, it would appear that God had forsaken Joseph. He had served the Lord and Potiphar with integrity, but it seemed God had "hung him out to dry." You do what is right at work and where does it get you? Not only fired, but imprisoned. Good cause for bitterness, isn't it? Well, Joseph didn't think so. He continued to live for the Lord as he always had. His circumstances may have changed, but his passion for God had not. And where was God in all of this? Right where He always was, in sovereign control, putting into motion the events that would ultimately shape world history. You see, God's ultimate plan was to move the Jewish people into a protected area of Egypt where they could multiply and grow into a mighty nation. When they reached the appropriate place of development, God allowed hardships upon them so their hearts would long to leave Egypt and return to the special land He had set aside for them. God used their exodus to bring incredible glory to Himself by miraculously parting the Red Sea, an event Jews still talked about centuries later.

How did Joseph fit into this grand plan? He was the man for the moment. Joseph was the man God used to start this process by getting this would-be nation into Egypt, which then consisted only of Joseph's family. But why prison for Joseph? Simple. It was one step closer to Pharaoh's (the king's) palace, which is where God ultimately placed Joseph. This wasn't any Egyptian prison. No, this was the prison used by Pharaoh himself. It was "the place where the king's prisoners were confined" (Genesis 39:19). It was also the place that God would use to further refine Joseph. It was where Joseph learned humility and absolute dependency on God — important traits that would serve him well when he became the second most powerful man in that part of the world.

Because of the lessons Joseph learned, he was prepared to take advantage of an enormous opportunity — an audience with the Pharaoh. Others in Joseph's position, when given this chance, would have used it to plead their innocence and beg to be freed. Not Joseph. He stayed focused on God. When Pharaoh asked him to interpret a dream, he quickly replied that only God could do that. Joseph was making God known to this very influential person. We know the rest of the story. Joseph explained that Pharaoh's dream meant Egypt would have seven years of abundance followed by a massive seven-year famine. He gave Pharaoh a plan to deal with the impending events, and Pharaoh made him second-in-command of the empire. Later, Joseph's family did bow to him, and he relocated them to Egypt, just as God had planned. Joseph had reached his *maxpoint*, which he describes to his brothers in Genesis 45:5-7: "And now, do not be distressed and do not be angry with yourselves for selling me here, because it was to save lives that God sent me ahead of you ... to preserve for you a remnant on earth and to save your lives by a great deliverance." Not bad for a former prisoner!

As a teenager, Joseph successfully completed the Decision Stage, determining that his life would focus on God. In his 20s, Joseph maneuvered through the Discovery Stage as he learned to obey the Lord in the midst of difficult circumstances. At 30, he entered the Deployment Stage with his life, making a significant impact on the lives of others. Seven years later, he moved into the Destiny Stage as he realized his *maxpoint*. Finally, at 110, he gave instructions for his body one day to be returned to his homeland. Joseph's work was now done, and his life ends ... mission accomplished.

Moses was much older than Joseph when he reached his *maxpoint*. This is not surprising, since Moses did not start his journey until he was 80. His Decision Stage began, oddly enough, in front of a burning bush that was not consumed. God spoke to Moses directly as He laid out His plan for Moses to lead the Jewish people out of Egyptian bondage. Moses did not welcome God's plan with open arms, to put it mildly. At that moment, Moses' plan for his life really did not align with God's. In fact, Moses could not remotely see himself doing what God saw him doing. He played every excuse card possible. Moses was at what Henry Blackaby calls in his book *Experiencing God,* "a crisis of belief." It was a battle of the wills between Moses and God. Eventually, Moses allowed God to empower him; he aligned his will with God's. Moses began to take action, moving himself and his family from the flocks of Midian back to Egypt. He entered the Discovery Stage as he started doing God's will.

The Discovery Stage, as we saw earlier, can be quite precarious. God, however, is faithful not to allow us to go through more than we can handle (1 Corinthians 10:13). We see this with Moses and the Israelites as they prepare to depart Egypt. Exodus 13:17-18 says, "When Pharaoh let the people go, God did not lead them on the road through the Philistine country, though that was shorter. For God said, 'If they face war, they might change their minds and return to Egypt.' So God led the people around by the desert road toward the Red Sea. The Israelites went up out of Egypt armed for battle." Even though they had *weapons* for war, God knew the Israelites did not have the *heart* for war. He gave them something they were better equipped to handle (crossing the Red Sea), which was still a stretch for them.

We glean some fascinating insights from Moses as he led the Israelite trek across the wilderness. The first is how he handled negative criticism. Moses repeatedly got an earful of it! In Exodus 16, the Israelites were letting him and Aaron have it over their lack of food. In verse 4, Moses heard from the Lord that He would provide them food. Moses responded to the people by telling them to prepare to see God's glory. God was about to work. He went on to say, "Who are we? You are not grumbling against us, but against the Lord." When criticized for doing God's will, Moses did not take it personally. He saw it as an opportunity to point people back to God.

The second lesson we learn from Moses is how he handled constructive criticism. Exodus 18 records a visit from Jethro, Moses' father-in-law, who had come to see firsthand all the miraculous things he had heard that God had done. He was excited about the report, but noticed something troubling. He watched as all day long people lined up before Moses so that he could judge their disputes. Jethro wisely observed that this was not good — Moses was wearing out. There was no way Moses could be a long-term, successful leader if he tried to micromanage everyone's problems. Moses needed help. He needed to delegate. He needed to raise up a team of leaders, and Jethro told him so. Verse 24 says, "Moses listened to his father-in-law and did everything he said." When you are given constructive criticism, do you get mad and defensive? Or, like Moses, do you have a teachable spirit that tries to learn from others? Do you try to do everything, or do you allow God to use others as well? Part of what God wants to teach us in the Discovery Stage is how to work together with other believers. It is not all about what I can accomplish, but what God can accomplish when two or more of His children agree to walk together.

Moses' journey with God may have started roughly, but their relationship quickly strengthened. This happened because Moses regularly spent time in God's presence, so much so that at one point his face shone from exposure to God's brightness. Moses, except for one incident, walked in obedience to God. He became totally dependent on Him, to the point that he told God, "If your presence does not go with us, do not send us up from here." (Exodus 33:15). He did not want to go anywhere without God.

If all you knew about Moses was Charlton Heston's rendition of him in the *Ten Commandments*, you might think Moses' *maxpoint* came at the crossing of the Red Sea. You would be mistaken. His *maxpoint* came in Exodus 20 and following when he delivered the Law of God to the Israelite people, and it continued as he regularly intervened to keep the Israelites from destruction.

It is amazing, when you stop to think about it, that the God of the Universe, Creator of heaven and earth, chose a man to deliver His message, His plan. An angel would not do. No, this message was too important to send through an emissary. It would be delivered by God himself to be passed on to generations to come by one man who had aligned his will with God's; one man who stepped out of his comfort zone to act upon God's Word; one man who was passionate about God and longed to spend time in His presence. It was Moses, a man who successfully journeyed to his *maxpoint*, but who also kept things in perspective.

You see, we are told in Numbers 12:3 that Moses was the humblest man in the world. Others had faithfully journeyed with God, but none with the humility of Moses. Pride could not be present in the man to whom God would hand his Law. No, God would have to receive all of the glory, and that is exactly what happened. The mission was accomplished.

Following in the footsteps of a well-admired leader is always difficult. Now imagine if it was a leader who had brought independence and deliverance to his people–a leader who all of the people respected because they knew he got his instructions firsthand from God. It was a legendary leader. That was the challenge placed before Joshua after the death of Moses.

In many ways, it would seem that Joshua's journey was simply a continuation of Moses' journey. The aide to Israel's deliverer was tapped by God to continue the process of returning the Israelites to their homeland in Canaan, or Palestine, as it is better known. It was a process that had been delayed 40 years because of the nation's unbelief and unwillingness to move into the land God told them to take. A new generation of Israelites emerged, with Joshua as leader, ready to take the mantle and accomplish what their parents would not.

Although Joshua held the same position Moses once had, their journeys were quite different. So it is with us. The journey God sets before us is as unique as our fingerprint, even if it intersects the paths that others have taken. We have our own cross to bear, our own decisions to make, and our own course to chart. We also will have to give our own account to God for it all.

We see Joshua, in the biblical book that bears his name, as a great military leader. We watch as he strategically moves his forces into the best positions to gain military victories. We marvel as one mighty city after another falls before his army. We cannot help but notice his dogged determination to stay the course until all of the Promised Land is conquered. But if you look behind the tough shell of this veteran warrior, you see someone who closely resembles what Twila Paris sang about in the song, *The Warrior is a Child*. You find that inside of a mighty warrior there is a child who needs rest and assurance.

Joshua was a man with childlike dependency on God, who passionately pursued the journey laid before him. When Moses left the scene, Joshua quickly stepped into his Deployment Stage. God had prepared Joshua for just such a moment. He had successfully completed the Decision and Discovery stages of his journey. Joshua's time had come.

We don't know how old Joshua was when he decided to align himself with God's will, but he must have been quite young. Moses trusted Joshua, I believe, because he saw in Joshua's heart something remarkably similar to his own. Exodus 33:11 says, "The Lord would speak to Moses face to face, as a man speaks with his friend. Then Moses would return to the camp, but his young aide Joshua, son of Nun, did *not leave the tent of meeting*." Moses would meet with God in a special tent outside the Israelite camp. Joshua would join him—but he didn't want to leave. Joshua wanted to stay in the Lord's presence. It is no wonder that when it came time to choose a successor to Moses, Joshua got the nod. "So the Lord said to Moses, 'Take Joshua, son of Nun, a man in whom is the spirit, and lay your hand on him" (Numbers 27:18).

Something interesting began to occur once Joshua entered his deployment zone. His influence and fame grew. First it was among his people, Israel. "That day the Lord exalted Joshua in the sight of all Israel; and they revered him all the days of his life, just as they had revered Moses" (Joshua 4:14). It is one thing to be the leader; it is quite another to have the respect of those you lead. God gave Joshua the respect of the people from that day forward, which was the day he successfully led them across the Jordan River into Palestine. It was an important day for Joshua when he went from merely holding the title of "leader" to actually becoming the leader.

I became a pastor when I was 23 years old. The pastor who preceded me was in his 60s. During my first year at that church, the title "pastor" was written on my office door, but it was not written on the hearts of the people. Brother Bob was still their pastor, even though Brother Bob now lived halfway across the country. It stayed that way until the church and I came to a "crossing the Jordan" experience. Those were tough days as we tackled problems, divisions, and other attacks from Satan; but in those days, I really became their pastor, as I led them through the difficult waters. That experience was in a small Midwestern church. I could only imagine what Joshua felt—and how relieved he was to have gotten the people's respect after the Jordan River.

God, however, had more in store for Joshua than the respect of his people, as significant as that was. He expanded Joshua's reputation throughout the region, gaining the respect of friend and foe alike. In Joshua 6:27, we read, "So the Lord was with Joshua, and his fame spread throughout the land." God went one step more by responding to him in a way He had never before or since done. He hearkened to Joshua's prayer that the sun would stand still so the Israelites could finish their battle with the Amorites. Joshua 10:14 tell us, "There has never been a day like it before or since, a day when the Lord listened to a man. Surely the Lord was fighting for Israel!"

Joshua's influence grew not only because of his famous acts, but also because of the encouragement he gave his followers. He had experienced God's strength. He had learned there is nothing to fear when God is on your side. Now he was able to exhort others to "... not be afraid; do not be discouraged. Be strong and courageous ..." (Joshua 10:25). This was the same message given to him several times when he assumed the leadership mantle. He had experienced it and was in a position to pass it to others.

The pattern that happened in Joshua's life is exactly what Peter talks about in 1 Peter 5:6 when he says, "Humble yourselves, therefore, under God's mighty hand, that He may lift you up in due time." In due time, Joshua was lifted up. He didn't seek fame. He never worried about being lost in Moses' shadow. He sought God and made sure he faithfully completed every assignment God gave.

Joshua reaches his *maxpoint* in chapter 11:21-23, when the land was finally conquered and peace prevailed. His ministry and influence continued as he divided the land, established cities of refuge, and gave a final challenge to the nation. Yes, Joshua was an awesome warrior, but deep inside the armor, the warrior was a child. He was a child who had complete faith and dependence on his Heavenly Father.

When Joshua was born, no one may have expected he would rise to greatness. However, there were others in Scripture from whom greatness was expected, whose birth had been predicted and whose parents were specially chosen. One such person was Samson.

From the beginning, Samson had everything going for him. The Angel of the Lord (believed by many scholars to be a pre-incarnate appearance of Christ) announced to his mother that he would be born. He would be special, the angel said, set apart to God from the time of his birth. Samson had great parents, the kind who loved him and sought God's wisdom in child rearing. In fact, after the angel announced Samson's coming birth, his father prayed that God would send the angel back to teach him how to raise the child (Judges 13:8). God had a great journey in mind for Samson. Unfortunately, he never made it. He had some accomplishments in his life, but they were nothing like they could have been. No, Samson never reached his *maxpoint*. He never fulfilled his destiny.

Instead of deciding to live his life for God's maximum glory, Samson lived for himself. He was the epitome of Cat Theology: It was all about him and his comfort. It was what he wanted, with no regard for others or God. He even had complete disregard for his Nazirite vow, which prevented him from cutting his hair, drinking anything that was fermented, and eating anything that was unclean. He violated all of it. We see that he was an angry man (Judges 14:19), a vengeful man (15:3, 7), and an immoral man (16:1). It is sad that in his death, he actually may have made his greatest impact (Judges 16:25-30).

Samson never learned to listen to the Lord, probably because he was too busy making his own noise. This is in stark contrast with another man born into a similar situation: Samuel. Like Samson, Samuel was set apart for the Lord even before conception (1 Samuel 1:11). He had a godly mother who literally gave him over to the Lord. He was taken to the priest to live in the House of the Lord as soon as he was weaned. Very early in his life, Samuel accomplished what Samson never did: he learned to listen to God.

We are told, "The Lord was with Samuel as he grew up, and he let none of his words fall to the ground. And all Israel … recognized that Samuel was attested as a prophet of the Lord" (1 Samuel 3:19-20). God spoke to Samuel and when Samuel spoke to others, God honored his words. Samuel stepped into his *maxpoint* in 1 Samuel 7:2-14 when he led Israel in a great revival and an impressive military victory, even though he never lifted the sword in battle. He later would be used by God to anoint Israel's first two kings. When I look at Samuel, I see a captain who is able to hold steady a mighty ship, no matter the storm.

Samson and Samuel were two men destined for greatness; unfortunately, only one made it. They were two men with a special calling, incredible parents, and great potential. Yet only one lived up to those things. How tragic yet typical of so many people. How many people never take the journey to their *maxpoint* because they simply will not listen to God? How many people shortchange their life's impact because they have become self-absorbed? How many people never learn to trust God because they won't leave their comfort zone?

Ultimately, what does it take to stay the course and become all that God would have you become? It takes an unshakable love for God. Our love for Him must be greater than our love for ourselves. Biblical David is a great example of how a godly love can enable one to overcome obstacles and stay the course. Whether it was running from King Saul or from his own son, Absalom, David maintained an unquenchable love for the Lord.

We have more insight into David's life than any other biblical character. We learn a lot about him before his name is even mentioned in the Bible. We first see that God had planned for David to lead Israel, and that he was a man after God's heart (1 Samuel 13:13-14). He was better than Saul (1 Samuel 15:28) and he had a pure heart (16:7). David already had his "to will" and "to do" lined up with God before he received his life's assignment. In fact, it was because of this God gave him the assignment He did— eventually to establish peace and protection for Israel.

Although God was prepared to have David rule Israel, David was not yet prepared for the role. It would take time, a lot of it, before he eventually would rule all Israel. Part of David's preparation involved living in two worlds—the world of a king and the world of a shepherd. After his anointing, but before it became public, David was recruited for public service. It seems he was quite the musician, and Saul's servants sought him out to play for the king whenever his spirit was troubled. Now here was David, one day in the palace and the next in the fields. One day he was playing for royalty, and the next moment he was sitting with dumb sheep. It was not an easy task, but one David performed with grace.

After the incident with Goliath and the development of a friendship with the king's son Jonathan, David would work full time in the palace. God was teaching David what it meant to be king by giving him this "internship." It seems it would be hard emotionally to function in such an environment—knowing you had been anointed king, which was still a secret to most of the world, and yet serving the very one you would replace. Yet David took it in stride; he served with excellence.

David was a remarkably patient man. He did not try to rush God's plan. He had an opportunity to kill Saul, which most would have considered justified, but he didn't take it. It wasn't God's timing, and David knew it. He would not get ahead of God. He would not try to reach his Destiny Stage or *maxpoint* until God said he was ready.

David approached his *maxpoint* in 2 Sam. 7:1-2 with his decision to try and build God a house, but took a huge detour when he sinned with Bathsheba. That act cost him greatly, but he repented and sought God's forgiveness. Eventually, he purchased the spot where the temple would be built (2 Sam. 24:18-25) and along the way, he prepared items for it (2 Sam. 8:7-11).

For all of his shortcomings—and they were many— David was an avid lover of God. He made some bad decisions and did not give enough attention to his family, but in his heart of hearts, he was sold out to God. His life clearly was more effective before his great sin than after. We can only wonder how much more effective David's life would have been had he not sinned with Bathsheba and later failed with his family. Yet David still made a difference, even after his fall, because of his love for God. It was that love that brought him to repentance, and it was that love that longed for God's approval above anyone or anything else.

Abraham, Joseph, Moses, Joshua, Samuel, and David — each a very different man with unique personalities, gifts, and callings, yet they all had one thing in common: they all reached their *maxpoint*. Samson and others faltered, but not these. Yes, there were distractions and detours. Yes, the journey was difficult at times. But no, they did not quit. They fixed their eyes on the Lord and ran for the goal — the goal of maximizing their lives for God's glory; the goal of making a difference in this world; the goal of leaving behind a legacy that positively impacted future generations. Can we do the same? Absolutely!

Think about it ...

Are you trying to short-cut your way to your *maxpoint*?

Have you, or are you currently, taking a detour away from the path that leads to your *maxpoint*?

What similarities do you see in your life when compared to Abraham? What about Joseph? Moses and Joshua? What about Samson and Samuel or David?

Chapter 6
God Uses Ordinary People

Abraham Lincoln reportedly said that God must really love ordinary people because He made so many of them. That's true, isn't it? God loves ordinary people. God loves everybody! God loves you! But sometimes, we feel we don't have what it takes to serve God. We look at great men like Abraham and David, Joshua and Joseph, and we feel that we just can't relate to them. "I could never be like them," we tell ourselves. "They were spiritual super heroes." Well, there is another character in Scripture that we can relate to. His name was Amos.

Now Amos was no entrepreneur like Abraham. He certainly wasn't a mighty warrior like Joshua or David. He did not have the royal upbringing of Moses or a prominent family like Joseph—nor did he have the religious training of Samuel. Amos was the least likely guy that you would expect to succeed in God's service. Amos certainly would not have been voted "most likely to succeed" by his senior class. If anything, it would have been the opposite. Amos was a *nobody*, but God used him to accomplish something great for Himself. Guess what? God wants to do the same with you!

There were four things about Amos with which we probably can relate. First, Amos had an insignificant home. Amos 1:1 tells us that he came from a place called Tekoa.

There was nothing particularly special about Tekoa. It is mentioned a couple times in Scripture, once referring to a wise woman from there (2 Samuel 14) and to workers from there, who helped Nehemiah rebuild Jerusalem's wall (Nehemiah 3). That is the extent of Tekoa's fame. It wasn't an important city by any means in Amos' day.

Tekoa was located about 12 miles southeast of Jerusalem in a desolate area of the Judean desert, close to the Dead Sea.[8] It may seem that 11 miles from Jerusalem to Tekoa is not very far, but in Israel, 11 miles can bring drastic geographical changes. Jerusalem has a high elevation, about 3,000 feet, where it can snow. As you leave Jerusalem heading southeast, you make a rapid descent to the Dead Sea, the lowest spot on earth. The climate drastically changes. This desert, desolate place called Tekoa is where Amos called home.

Second, we see that Amos had an insignificant job. In Amos 7:14 it says that he was a shepherd, and he tended sycamore-fig trees. So, Amos actually worked two jobs, neither very significant in the eyes of most people. He took care of sheep and cared for trees which produced a type of fruit that only the poorest people ate. There was nothing particularly exciting about Amos' work. This is not exactly the career parents would dream for their child. We may feel we are like Amos and stuck in an insignificant job. But the truth is that God can use you right where you are, whether or not you think what you do is significant. God can use you to impact this world for Jesus Christ.

---

[8] Tenney, M., gen. ed., *Zondervan's Pictorial Bible Dictionary* (1998), Zondervan: Grand Rapids; page 829.

Lech Walesa probably didn't see his job in the shipyard as all that significant. Lech lived in Communist Poland, but he had a dream in his heart. It was the dream of freedom. Lech led a labor protest and lost his job over it. For four years, he moved between insignificant, odd jobs. Then he began to organize a union solidarity movement that eventually led to the toppling of the Communist government. Lech was elected president in Poland's first general election after more than 40 years under Communist dictatorships. He started with an insignificant job, but became his nation's leader.[9]

Amos also had an insignificant education. In chapter 7, verse 14, Amos says, "I was neither a prophet nor a prophet's son ..." He had not been to prophet's school, but that is what he became. He had no formal training in religious leadership. Many would argue that he was not qualified to fulfill the role in which he found himself, but that did not matter to God, who does not judge by man's criteria.

A few months after I became a pastor, the church had its annual "fall revival." The deacons scheduled a speaker before I had been called there. This man, who also was a pastor, had very little education. His grammar was poor and his pulpit presence awkward. Yet the hand of God was on him. We saw God move in incredible ways in the hearts of people. Many lost people came to Christ through this man's preaching. Like Amos, God used this man, despite his lack of training ... Now, don't misunderstand. Training and education are important. It is helpful to be

---

[9] Source: http://www.president.pl/dflt/en_hisprez.php3.

well equipped to be the best servant possible. But a lack of training should not keep us from seeking to become all God wants us to be.

In addition to formal training, we notice that Amos had insignificant experience. He said that he was not the son of a prophet. His daddy wasn't a preacher, and he certainly had no experience as one. God used him anyway. How many times do we use our lack of experience as an excuse not to attempt great things for God?

Michael Cooper and I were sitting at a restaurant in the Dallas-Ft. Worth Airport, eating sandwiches while we waited for our flight. We were headed to Romania, and this was Michael's first mission trip. He confessed to me how intimidated he was when he initially considered going. Our plan was to spend an entire week sharing the gospel house to house, trusting God to draw people to Himself.

Michael had little experience at this. He had only led one person to faith in Christ since becoming a Christian several years prior, and that person was his daughter. As he prepared for the trip by memorizing Scripture and practicing his witnessing "technique," God began to give him confidence.

Between bites of Texas barbecue, he shared how much his faith had grown as he got ready for the trip. Michael thought it would take a few days, but he expected that by Thursday of the week we were there, he would be able to lead someone to Christ. Michael was wrong.

At the first Romanian house Michael visited, he led the family to Christ. There was no gospel witness in the village Michael worked. No church that proclaimed salvation through faith in Christ. As far as we knew, no one before Michael and his little team had ever shared God's love with those residents. God used Michael, someone with little witnessing and no missions experience, to actually start a cell church there.

So, how do you get experience? Simple. You jump in and do it. Make yourself available to God and go for it. Michael did, and since that first trip, he has been on several others, each time becoming more effective for Christ. He is now a faithful witness who looks for creative ways to share Christ with co-workers and others who he meets.

Ida emigrated from China to the United States as a child. Ida is a homemaker. She didn't have any special skills, education or experience, but she wanted to be used by God. She went to Brazil on a missions trip, and soon found herself right at home sharing Christ with the Brazilians. In the course of a week, this woman led close to 30 people to Christ and helped start a new church. Insignificant? Hardly.

Like Michael and Ida, Amos also experienced significance in his life once he let God take control. First, God gave Amos a significant calling. Amos in 7:15 says, *"The Lord took me from tending the flock."* There was Amos in the back side of the desert, minding his own business, when God got a hold of him. God took him, and called him to do something great. He called him to be a prophet.

We often think of a prophet as someone who predicts the future. A prophet's job, however, was to tell forth the Word of God, which sometimes included details of future events. Their ministry was to stand against sin and call nations to repentance. God called Amos to be His spokesman. He wanted Amos to stand in the gap and speak against sin.

In Amos' day, Israel was divided into two nations. The first, called Israel, or the Northern Kingdom, was comprised of 10 Jewish tribes in the north. The other, Judah, included the remaining two southern tribes. Amos was sent from his home in Judah to be a missionary to the Northern Kingdom, although he also had a ministry in his country and some surrounding nations. At this particular time, both North and South were experiencing great prosperity. Their economies were booming. Their militaries were strong; but, spiritually, they had hit an all-time low. When it came to righteousness, they were bankrupt.

God raised up Amos to take a message to the especially depraved North. "What you are doing is wrong. It is ungodly. You must do something about it!" Amos did not mince words with Israel's leadership. He called sin what it was. He didn't call it mistakes, slips or errors in judgment; he called it sin. Pretty bold for an uneducated, inexperienced man from the back side of the desert! This was a significant responsibility.

God had more in store for Amos. He gave Amos a significant audience to deliver his message to: the city of Bethel. Bethel was the cultural center of Israel. It was where the educated and the elite lived. Bethel was a trend-setting place, and that is where God sent Amos. They had their own false prophets and religious leaders, and Amos came nose to nose with one of them, Amaziah. Amaziah had all the schooling and religious credentials that Amos lacked. But that did not matter. Amos had a significant audience and he took advantage of it.

God also gave Amos a significant determination. In verse 7:12, *"Amaziah said unto Amos, 'Oh thou seer...'"* — which means a prophet for hire. To him, Amos was nothing more than a religious mercenary. *"Go flee into the land of Judah, and there eat bread and prophesy there."* Amaziah told Amos to get lost. Instead of turning and running, Amos held his ground with great determination and responded with a word from God. Amos was not a quitter. He did not throw in the towel when things started to get uncomfortable. He was determined that even if he had to stand alone, he was going to stand.

Finally, Amos had been given significant boldness. He got in Amaziah's face and said, *"This is what God says, your wife is going to be a prostitute."* That's pretty bold! *"And your sons and daughters are going to die by the sword, and the land is going to be divided up, it's going to be conquered."* No mincing words here ... he boldly delivered God's message.

Yes, God does use ordinary people ... ordinary people who yield control of their lives to God; ordinary people who exchange their will for God's will; ordinary people who step out in obedience. He uses ordinary people who faithfully complete whatever assignment He gives them, no matter how great or seemingly insignificant.

Don't let excuses keep you from serving God. Don't spend your time focusing on what you don't have. Rather, focus on what you do have as a believer: the Holy Spirit living in you. You have the power of Almighty God resting upon you. You have the call, concern, and course set for you from the Lord. You have the promise of Jesus

Christ never to leave you nor forsake you and to be with you to the end of the age. It doesn't get any better than that! Step out in obedience to God and let Him make you into someone extraordinary.

Think about it ...

What are you doing that is significant?

How do you see yourself? Is this how God views you?

How are you like Amos? How are you different?

In what unique way do you think God might use your life?

Chapter 7
Alka-Seltzer Christians

For many years, Alka-Seltzer, the heartburn and pain relief medicine, used the slogan "Plop, plop, fizz, fizz, oh what a relief it is." The slogan mimicked what happened when you used the medicine. You plop two tablets into a glass of water, which immediately starts to fizz. To be most effective, you are supposed to drink it while it is still fizzing. If left alone, the tablets eventually fizzle out and are of little use …

Unfortunately, there are many Christians who are like those Alka-Seltzer tablets. They go strong for a while and then fizzle out. The reality is that all of us, at any point along our journey, are in danger of fizzling out. The mission is precarious, and as we saw in the last chapter, there are extreme pressures working against us. We haven't even mentioned that Satan, like a roaring lion, would like nothing more than to devour us and sift us like wheat. The landscape of Christianity is littered with people, some of whom were once great leaders, who have self-destructed. They attained great heights, maybe even reached their *maxpoint*, but blew it.

This is what happened to Gideon. God called Gideon to deliver the Israelites from the Midianites who were oppressing Israel during the days of the judges. You recall the story of how Gideon's 300-man militia overcame the

100,000-man fighting force of the Midianites. It must have been quite a sight as Gideon's forces, armed only with trumpets and torches, subdued this massive army.

You may remember that Gideon got into this whole thing rather reluctantly. I imagine he could hardly keep from laughing when the angel of the Lord appeared and called him a "mighty warrior" (Judges 6:11). After all, "mighty" and "warrior" were definitely not the first two words that popped into people's minds when they thought of Gideon. They surely weren't what Gideon thought of himself. In fact, when the angel approached, Gideon was secretly threshing wheat, hoping those dreaded Midianites would not find and steal it. He was an unlikely candidate, but God used him anyway.

"Now for the rest of the story," as radio host Paul Harvey would say. What happened after Gideon's great victory? He fizzled. When we find Gideon approaching the end of his life, he had turned his back on God, and led the children of Israel away from the Lord. How could this happen?

Notice first that Gideon started strong. The odds were against him, but he won. He overcame tremendous obstacles—not just the Midianites, but obstacles within Israel. Judges chapters seven and eight tell us that when Gideon's 300 men began to rout the Midianites, Gideon called for reinforcements from the various Israelite tribes. He said, "We have got them on the run. Now come and cut them off." There were, however, some leaders of the tribe of Ephraim who were upset they hadn't been included in the initial attack. They verbally let Gideon have it, disgusted that they had been left out.

Gideon was criticized by God's people for doing what God told him to do. Warren Samuels, a former pastor who is now president of Next Worldwide Ministries, calls this "sheep bites." He says sheep bites, which come from Christians, hurt far more than wolf bites, which come from the unsaved. Gideon did not let the sheep bites distract him. He tactfully talked to Ephraim's leaders, "Isn't it better to have been a part of extending the victory than just participating in the initial attack? After all, it was you guys who captured the Midianite leaders. That is much nobler than what little I did." With great wisdom, Gideon moved beyond their unfounded criticism.

Gideon did something else that was right. He prevented Israel from making him their king. Notice Judges 8:22.

> "The Israelites said to Gideon, 'Rule over us – you, your son and your grandson – because you have saved us out of the hand of Midian.' But Gideon told them, 'I will not rule over you, nor will my son rule over you. The Lord will rule over you.'"

The people got caught in the emotions of victory and offered to make Gideon a political dynasty. Gideon turned them down. He refused this prestigious position for himself and his family because it was wrong. God wanted to be the king of Israel, the one to whom Israel would look for direction and support. Gideon understood that. The only reason God later relented and gave kings to Israel was because of their rebellion.

So far, Gideon was doing pretty well. The fizz, however, was about to start dissipating. In his next breath after turning down the kingship, Gideon asked the people to bring him some of the gold earrings they plundered from the Midianites. The people gladly responded and gave Gideon 43 pounds of gold.[10] So what is the problem with Gideon doing this? Partaking in the fruits of victory seems innocent enough. Gideon, however, was actually flirting with temptation.

It was common in that day for heathen nations to melt the precious metals seized from their military victories and make idols. Gideon melted the gold and made a trophy commemorating his victory that Israel eventually worshipped. This sin, like so many others, started as a seemingly innocent temptation. Isn't this exactly how it usually works? Satan does not walk up to you and say, "I want you to sin! I want you to ruin your life; I want you to throw away everything that is good and abort this journey toward making a maximum impact. I want you to self-destruct."

Temptation itself is not sin. It was not wrong for Gideon to take that gold or even to melt it down into a trophy. There was nothing inherently wrong in that act. The problem, however, was that trophy represented a temptation to idolatry. It was a temptation to take credit for a victory that was actually God's. It was a temptation to place the focus of future trust on something material rather than in God. It was a temptation to which Gideon succumbed.

---

[10] Source: NIV footnote on Judges 8:26.

Sin is nothing with which to flirt. Seemingly innocent situations can quickly turn to compromise if we are not careful. This is why God exhorts us to "abstain from all appearance of evil," (1 Thessalonians 5:22 KJV). We are to flee from evil, not flirt with it. 1 Corinthians 6:18 tells us to flee sexual immorality. 1 Corinthians 10:14 says to flee idolatry. 1 Timothy 6:11 admonishes us to flee quarreling, discontentment, and the love of money. 2 Timothy 2:22 warns us to flee the evil desires of youth. When Joseph was put in a compromising position with his boss's wife, he fled.

As if things were not bad enough with Gideon, he passes on this temptation to others. He doesn't just keep this "trophy" to himself; he erects it in his city so everyone can see it and be tempted by it. Sure enough, the trophy became quite an attraction in Israel and people began coming from all over the country to see it. Next thing you know, they were worshipping this hunk of metal that originally was just a war memorial. In many of our cities, we will find war memorials. Imagine if the next one you saw was surrounded by people bowing to worship it. That was the scene in Gideon's hometown of Ophrah.

Gideon flirted with temptation. It took its course, and he fell into sin. Once that occurred, sin did three things. It reversed Gideon, it ensnared Gideon, and it multiplied through Gideon. Shortly before this, Gideon was trusting God. He was obedient. He was leading the charge for the people of God. Sin reversed all of that; it reversed Gideon. Now instead of praising God, he was worshipping a lifeless statue.

Sin can reverse us as well. Sin can cause people who were once happy, joyous, and excited about the things of God to revert to being cold, bitter, and self focused. People who trusted God for everything now look for deliverance no farther than their bank account, career or education. Individuals who faithfully attended church now use Sundays as a day to wax their boat or practice their golf swing. Sin has reversed them. Like Gideon, the object of their worship is no longer God, but something made by the hands of men.

When we give in to sin, our thinking is clouded. We begin to lose our sense of moral direction as we quench the Holy Spirit's conviction. It is like putting a magnet next to a compass: we no longer can find true north.

Sin also ensnared Gideon. His 43-pound trophy became a trap to him and his family. Like a rat caught in a trap, Gideon took the bait and was now ensnared in sin. Like an ocean riptide, he found himself being pulled deeper and deeper into sin. Much like Gideon's experience, in our Christian walk, one sin quickly leads to another until you become trapped.

Finally, sin multiplied through Gideon. Before anyone knew it, all of Israel was following his example. It's important for us to remember that our sin affects others. We have phrases in our culture like "victimless crimes" and "consenting adults," phrases that imply your actions did not affect anyone but yourself. Don't buy into the lie. Sin has a rippling effect that often devastates those you love most.

What can we do to avoid being Alka-Seltzer Christians? How can we avoid the ravaging effects of sin? What can we do to stay on course? Here are four simple reminders that can be profoundly beneficial.

First, stay in the Word. There is an old saying that goes, "the Bible will keep you from sin and sin will keep you from the Bible." David said in Psalm 119:105, "Your word is a lamp to my feet and a light for my path." God's Word will show us right from wrong. God's Word will keep us from succumbing to temptation.

Second, communicate with God. It is pretty hard to live in sin when you consistently talk to the Savior. Prayer brings us into God's presence, and once there, we are compelled to cry out with Isaiah, "Woe to me … for I am a man of unclean lips, and I live among a people of unclean lips, and my eyes have seen the King, the Lord Almighty."

Third, avoid temptation whenever possible. Many times, we put ourselves into tempting situations that we could have avoided. I read a story about a captain of an oil tanker who made regular runs from South America to Los Angeles. One day, he was approached by drug smugglers who offered him $10,000 to take a load of drugs from Latin America to California. The captain refused. A few days later, the drug runners returned. This time they offered him $50,000 for a one-time run. The captain again refused. Not to be dissuaded, the bootleggers came back and upped the ante to $150,000. Again, the skipper refused, but this time, he called the authorities.

The FBI set up a "sting" operation that resulted in the seizure of several tons of drugs, $340,000 in cash and the names of the Los Angeles-area drug dealers with whom this gang was working. After the operation was completed, one of the FBI agents asked the captain why he had waited to contact them until the bounty was at $150,000.00. The captain replied, "It is because they were getting very close to my price and I was getting scared."

That captain realized that he had a limit. He knew the power of temptation. Ten thousand dollars was not a temptation to him, but $150,000 was pretty close. He got out just in time. Knowing when to get out and move away from temptation is critical to avoiding the traps of sin. Putting safeguards in place to keep us from temptation is also very beneficial.

Lastly, destroy any sin that creeps into your life. Don't let it fester. Don't give the devil a stronghold in your life. When the Holy Spirit convicts you of sin, confess it to the Lord, repent, and move away from it. When it comes to sin, our mission is to seek and destroy.

When the book on Gideon's life came to a close, we no longer saw him as a great servant of God. The mighty warrior of the Lord had vanished. What was left in his place was a spiritual has-been. We saw a man who was causing more spiritual harm than good. We saw a sad and troubling train wreck and were reminded that any of us could easily have something similar happen.

Gideon, like all of us, was called to swim against the flow of sin, not get caught up into it. When I think about this truth, I am reminded of one of the most unique experiences I have had: swimming in the Dead Sea. There's nothing quite like the Dead Sea anywhere in the world. It is called the Dead Sea because there's nothing living in it. What is especially interesting about it is its salt content, which is about 33 percent. Compare that with the oceans, which have a salt content of four percent. The effect of this is that you cannot sink in the Dead Sea, even if you don't know how to swim. The dense salt content acts just like a life vest. It holds you up!

It was a weird feeling trying to turn around or roll over onto my back while swimming there. These normally simple maneuvers were suddenly very difficult. The same salt content that kept you up also made it difficult to move. It was akin to salmon trying to swim upstream. The flow of the river pushes against them, trying to drive them in the opposite direction and drag them away from their intended destination.

We live in a society that is very much like the Dead Sea or the river driving against the salmon. Everything around us tries to push us back, to drive us away from intimacy with Christ. The pressure is on to abort the pursuit of our *maxpoint*. Yet, in the midst of all this, God calls us to go against the flow. God calls us to rise above the pressures of evil and excel for the Lord Jesus Christ. How is this possible? Do we even know what pressures we are really up against?

We find the answers to these questions in a conversation that Christ had with His disciples recorded in Chapter 8 of the Gospel of Mark. We often refer to this exchange as "Peter's Confession." Jesus said to his disciples,

> *"Who do people say I am?' They replied, 'Some say John the Baptist; others say Elijah; and still others, one of the prophets.' 'But what about you?' he asked. Who do you say that I am?' Peter answered, 'You are the Christ'"* (27-29).

This exchange between Christ and His disciples took place at Caesarea Philippi, on the northeastern corner of the Sea of Galilee. It's about 120 miles from Jerusalem, and just 50 miles from Damascus, Syria, in the area known today as the Golan Heights. What is significant about this place is that in Jesus' time, it was a very pagan area. Good Jews did not live on that side of the Sea of Galilee. They lived on the western side. The heathens lived in Caesarea Philippi. The Jews living there would have been so "Helenized," or indoctrinated to Greek culture, that you could not tell they were Jews. They lost their identity. They stopped their worship of Jehovah God. They blended into a pagan society.

In Jesus' day, Caesarea Philippi had a temple erected in honor of the god Pan. Its worship sessions were very hedonistic. Pan worship, by the way, continues among modern pagans. It was in this incredibly pagan setting that Christ asked his disciples, "Who do people say that I am?"

One of the pressures we face on our journey is a pagan society. A flip of the television, a drive past the theater marquee, even a commute to work past billboards reveals how pagan our society has become. Righteousness is mocked while immorality and debauchery are exalted. Public arena battles rage, as the forces of evil seek to drive out anything of God from the public square. Yet, in the midst of all this, we are called to rise above the tide. We are expected to swim against the flow of garbage that seeks to pummel us.

There is another kind of pressure that Christ identified in his questioning: peer pressure. It was a relevant question then to ask what the disciples' peers thought of

Christ, and it is a relevant question today. Some people say he was a lunatic or fanatic. Some deny he even lived, while others dismiss him as irrelevant or see him as a crutch for the weak. You may even be under the pressure of family, neighbors or co-workers who deny Christ's true identity. It certainly is a challenging place to be, since our peers often have such a strong influence in our lives. The younger we are, the more it seems that this is an issue. We want to be liked. We want to fit in with those around us. The issue of Christ's identity, however, may make this difficult at best and nearly impossible at worst.

There is a third pressure identified in this passage: our pride. We see this in an exchange that Peter has with Christ. After Peter's great confession, Jesus began to explain to the disciples how He would have to suffer and die. Peter did not like what he was hearing and actually rebuked Christ. Can you imagine that? I would guess that Peter said something like this:

"Come here, Lord. Come over here where we can have a private conversation. Now Jesus, you've got these things all mixed up. You don't need to be doing it this way. What you're supposed to do is go into Jerusalem and proclaim yourself the king. Drive out those nasty Romans and set up your kingdom with us ruling at your side. I don't want to hear any more nonsense about this suffering business."

Peter had his pride. He had his own way of doing things, and he was bold enough to tell Jesus. Now before you fault Peter too much, ask yourself this question: Don't we often act the same way? Don't we have our own way that we think God should work? Don't we try to plan everything and then ask God to bless it? Just like in the case of the cross, God may have another way He wants to work that we cannot even conceive.

Jews in Jesus' day were looking for a temporal king. They thought the Messiah would deliver them from Roman oppression and bring back the glory days of Israel. They did not understand the Messiah first had to come as a spiritual king to make atonement for the sins of this world before he would one day come as a political king and rule the world.

Peter's plan was for Jesus to sidestep the cross, which is why Jesus replied to him, *"Get behind me, Satan."* Peter was trying to get Christ to do the same thing the devil had tried when he tempted Christ in the wilderness. Jesus had a better plan. It would not be a "quick fix" but an eternal solution to man's greatest disease: sin. Like Peter, we wrestle with pride and pressure, but we cannot allow it to drag us down, causing us to miss the perfect plan of God.

The real question is: How do we rise above all these pressures? The answer is our personal confession. Peter did acknowledge Jesus for who He was, even though he had a different opinion about what he should do. He was the Christ, the Messiah, the Savior sent to redeem the world. We also must come to a time and a point in our lives when we accept Jesus Christ as our Lord and our Savior. This is the point where we turn away from our sin and place our trust in Christ and Christ alone for the forgiveness of our sin. There is no hope apart from a *personal* confession of Jesus Christ. It cannot be your spouse's, your parents' or your children's. It has to be yours. You may think you are on the journey to your *maxpoint*, but if this issue isn't settled, you are not.

Once that is taken care of, we need to have a perfected outlook if we are going to swim successfully against the stream. We need to see things differently than we are accustomed. Notice what Jesus told Peter in verse 33, "You do not have in mind the things of God, but the things of men." Peter was not focusing on the things above. He was only looking to the moment.

No matter what stage of the journey we are in, we can quickly slide backwards if we take our eyes off of Christ. If we let our affections wander to the things of this world, we can easily become sidetracked. We will get sucked into the pressures of society, our peers, and pride if we do not take captive our thoughts and direct them heavenward. This is a continual battle that we will face our entire life.

As long as there is sin in the world, there will always be a pagan society seeking to sweep us away. As long as there are people without Christ, there will be pressure to move away from the Lord. As long as we are on this side of Heaven, we will have to wrestle with our pride. The good news is that we can be victorious, thanks to the work of Christ on the cross. We can swim against the stream because, "greater is He that is in you then he that is in the world." We are more than conquerors through Him who loved us.

Think about it ...

Are you in any way flirting with sin?

How is your prayer life?

Do you spend time each day in God's word?

Do you feel pressured to sin or quit pursuing your *maxpoint*? Are you giving in to those pressures?

Chapter 8
What is Your *Maxpoint?*

At the pinnacle of his career, Roy Frady ranked in the top 1 ½ percent of Hollywood's highest paid actors. The native of Houston, TX, landed in Hollywood following several years as a successful stage and TV actor in England, Canada, and the U.S. Roy enjoyed the good life that his acting career afforded him. He had just been offered a five-picture contract with an international film company. Amid the fans and world travel, somehow Roy lacked peace and significance. Increasingly, he became dissatisfied with the self-centeredness of "Tinseltown" and what he felt was prostitution of his craft. Roy and his wife, Sandra, were hungry for something more.

One day, during a weekly golf game, as Los Angeles smog placed a shadow over the seventh green, something clicked inside of Roy. Soon after, he left Hollywood and his acting career, and he and Sandra moved to Houston where they began attending church.

The pastor's sermons penetrated Roy and reconnected him to the spiritual journey he had begun as a boy.

A downturn in the U.S. economy during the early 1980s precipitated an unexpected career change. Roy reentered the workforce in the unlikely field of engineering. Over eight years — while simultaneously attending seminary and raising a family—Roy earned a great living as vice president for three major engineering firms.

In 1990, Roy's tireless motivation for higher levels of success—coupled with his family's history of heart disease—caught up with him. Roy had a heart attack that forced him to slow down. Though he struggled to hold on to the fast pace of his successful engineering career, eventually he yielded to God's calling on his life. After his recovery, Roy began speaking evangelistically in small and obscure churches, prisons, and nursing homes—and pretty much anywhere people would listen. "Small" and "obscure" were new concepts for Roy, considering the large crowds he had measured his success by as an actor. In 1993, Roy opened his first church, transforming an old movie theater into a congregation that served people no one else wanted.

Over the years, Roy grew wise to the *narcotic* of pursuing material success, which "demanded a little more each time to reach that initial high." Today, Roy has found contentment in God. His new measure of success consists of striving to become less while depending more on God. He has added services as police and fire chaplain to his duties as a pastor. In Roy's surrender to full-time ministry, he began the journey towards his *maxpoint*. He wrestled with the question, "Who or what will I live for?" and correctly chose God. As an actor, Roy's focus was temporal. His vision was shortsighted. That all changed when he moved into the Decision Stage. Roy aligned his will with God's will as he learned to focus on what really mattered. Roy Frady no longer desires to play to fans numbering in the thousands—but to an Audience of One.

Todd Szalkowski and his wife Amy were wealthy, young professionals who lived for golf, traveling and their six-figure income. Then in 1994, a career-building move to work for a Dallas-based tax accounting firm found them living in new surroundings and hearing something Todd hadn't heard in years—God's voice.

While Todd was in college 10 years before, his heart was softened toward the gospel from hearing the testimony of a dorm neighbor. Soon afterward, Todd attended a church in Athens, GA, and placed his faith in God once he understood Christ died for his sins. Though Todd's faith grew through regular participation in church and campus ministry during his sophomore year, little by little, the lure of campus night life eclipsed his nascent faith—but not forever.

When Todd and Amy moved to Dallas around the mid nineties, immediately they plugged into a church, where one of Todd's new colleagues attended. Before long, Todd began teaching Sunday school, and Amy sang in the choir. During an annual Christmas store outreach, Amy and other church volunteers would help underprivileged parents acquire gifts for their families. In an adjacent room, Todd counseled the shoppers and witnessed the Holy Spirit bring several people to Christ through Todd's seemingly inadequate presentations of the gospel.

Then, in 2001, Todd stepped out in faith, accepting a challenge from his pastor to attend a weeklong mission trip to Trujillo, Peru. Like before, Todd felt unqualified as an evangelist of the gospel; he had never even written down his testimony. God faithfully removed Todd's doubt through a woman who "regained" her sight. During the mission, Todd gave the woman a $10 pair of eyeglasses he bought at a 7-Eleven that he'd unconsciously tucked away in his travel bag. The eyeglasses brought tears of joy and restored the woman's vision, which—unbeknownst to Todd—enabled her to return to a ministry leadership position she had lost. Like never before, Todd saw God's power to use him—regardless of his performance or scriptural knowledge.

Later, a financial stewardship course convicted Todd and Amy to be faithful to God with more than just the 10-percent sliver off the top of their earnings. Subsequently, they eliminated existing debt and began placing their finances in God's hands to freely help those who needed it most—something they never before conceived of doing. In 2004, Todd resigned from his position as partner at the tax accounting firm to become a church planter for a Texas-based international mission organization. Instead of bringing in a six-figure salary to achieve material wealth for their family, today Todd and Amy have relinquished control of their income. They have entrusted their livelihood to God, who—through the hands of faithful donors—provides every penny they need. Todd and Amy have never felt as secure as they do today by relying on God's help to guide them.

When Todd and Amy connected with the Dallas-area church, they began to discover more and more of God's expectations for their lives. As they studied His word and started teaching it themselves, they realized they could not simply hear the Word—they had to do it. In the Discovery Stage, Todd and Amy learned a lot about themselves. They began to see that God could use them—whether by working in an outreach "store" or giving a pair of reading glasses to a Peruvian. They learned the importance of consistent obedience and they discovered God's faithfulness. Todd and Amy earned six figures but were none the richer. Now, they have riches and security that money can't buy.

Gary Pettet has been devoted to pulling people from fiery flames for more than 20 years. First, he served as a lieutenant of a Cleveland-area fire department and then, as an impassioned church planter with a global missions ministry.

Gary didn't always possess the sort of courage that risks life and limb to save others. He grew up in an unsupportive home run by an alcoholic father who produced a young man with low self-esteem and addictions to alcohol and drugs. At age 18, Gary was arrested for smoking marijuana with minors, but later was released by a cop who gave him a second chance cemented in a strong warning, "I don't ever want to see you again!"

While working a small job with a vending company, Gary was smitten with a laundromat clerk on his route. She refused Gary's invitations to lunch, but countered with an invitation to her church, where Christians were praying Gary would become desperate for Christ's love and forgiveness. Gary accepted the invitation and heard the gospel at her church. Several days later, at the age of 19, he mouthed a simple prayer of salvation: "God, if you are real, come into my life." Cigarettes he had been packing in a vending machine shot out everywhere, as his body quaked and then filled with an unexplainable peace and joy. The miraculous change in Gary's morality and work habits were a convincing witness.

Gary soon left the vending company and entered the medical field, first as a dialysis technician and then as a paramedic student. Eventually, Gary was hired as a fire fighter in a small Ohio town where 50 men responded to 1,500 fires, vehicle accidents, traumas, and illnesses each year. God used the position to build courage in Gary from the fractured building blocks of his teenage years. Risking his life for the safety of others became a daily requirement. Gary met the tests with audible utterances of faith by sharing scriptures while administering CPR.

When I first met Gary and his wife Darla, I was impressed with their solid faith and Christian work ethic. They gave one-hundred percent to everything they did — their jobs, church, and raising three boys. In 1999, I invited Gary and Darla to join me for a mission trip to Romania where we saw many people come to Christ. That event eventually sparked Gary's movement into the Deployment Stage.

After the Romania experience, returning to the fire department seemed like taking backward steps on the journey to spiritual significance. Though, as a fireman, Gary ministered to and held the hands of many people who breathed their last breaths, he was unsure of the impact he was having on eternity. However, one thing Gary knew is that he loved seeing people come to Christ. After 20 years of serving the fire department — the last five of which he served as lieutenant — Gary resigned with distinction: He had never lost a fire fighter in the line of duty.

Now, each year Gary and Darla travel to various countries to plant churches and open medical clinics, so they can exercise their gifts of compassions on physically and spiritually needy people. God is deploying them in ways that are growing His kingdom. Gary has focus and specificity to his ministry. He is seeing his life make a lasting impact on others. As a bold evangelist of the gospel at age 49, Gary has journeyed far from the days of low self-esteem and self-loathing to find confidence and maximum fulfillment in the one true God. As he continues to rescue lives—this time for eternity—Gary finds himself on a trajectory towards his *maxpoint*.

It was a fitting moment in what would become a monumental week for me. I was standing in the wrestling gym at the U.S. Olympic Training Center in Colorado Springs when something arrested my attention. As our tour guide explained the workout regimens for Olympic wrestlers, my focus shifted to a poster hanging on the wall beside us. It showed the 2000 Olympic gold metal wrestler Brandon Slay kneeling on one knee pad. An inscription made in pen was visible on the other knee pad: "Psalm 144:1." In the bottom right of the poster was Slay's signature and the words, "Search for the Greater Gold." Coming from a man who had reached the pinnacle of success for his sport, *Search for the Greater Gold*, is a powerful message that there is more to life than gold medals or a successful career. The *greater gold* can only be found in a life that belongs to Christ. It is also a message, I believe, about the importance of not settling for the moment. It is an encouragement to become all that God would have you to be—to reach for your *maxpoint*.

This was a fitting moment for me because it came during a week when God was speaking to my heart about my future—the journey to my own *maxpoint*. I was in Colorado Springs for meetings of a ministry board that I served. I had some downtime between that meeting and others that I had on behalf of the missions agency for which I worked. I was able to visit the Olympic training center, but more importantly, I was able to spend some extra alone time with God. It was in those moments with God, with the gorgeous scenery of the majestic Colorado Rockies as a backdrop, that I heard both a question and a statement from God. While not audible, God's words to me were just as clear.

First, the question, "How can a person impact the world hundreds of years after his death?" I thought about Martin Luther and the words he wrote sparking the Reformation. I pondered the impact of those writings today. Then my thoughts shifted to a contemporary writer, Henry Blackaby, and how he had impacted my life even though I had never met him. I quickly became convinced that one answer to God's question, at least for me, was writing. I made the decision that May day in 2003 to start writing.

Later that week came the statement from God, "It is now okay for you to focus on your personal development and dreams. Start by finishing your master's degree." That statement was significant because I had spent the preceding five years giving everything I had to the missions agency I was serving. When I left the pastorate, I put on hold the master's degree work I was doing so that I could devote my energies to the agency. My dreams all centered on the organization where I worked—seeing it grow and reach its full potential. I hadn't given a lot of thought to what *my* full potential might be. I didn't dream a lot about what I could do for Christ—not like I used to dream as a teenager when God first called me to vocational ministry. No, my dreams were for the organization and for what God could do in others.

Now, don't misunderstand, there is nothing wrong with that. In fact, you should dream for what your church, ministry, and other people can become. But you also have to dream for yourself. You have to dream about your *maxpoint*. You have to dream about what God wants you to become. You have to dream about making a broad and lasting impact with your life for God's glory.

I returned home from Colorado Springs with a commitment to finish seminary, write a book, and pursue the dream of making a lasting and global impact for the cause of Christ. A year later, almost to the day, I graduated from seminary, you are now reading the book I committed to write, and I am pursuing the dream as I now live in the Destiny Stage. My desire is to focus the rest of my life on spiritual multiplication, not just addition.

Multiplication of ministry is a key component of the Destiny Stage. Another word that could be used instead of multiplication is *leverage*. You are leveraging a little to accomplish a lot. Honestly, many people, even those in vocational ministry, don't think much about leverage or multiplication. They live for the moment—not necessarily because they want to—but because they have allowed the "tyranny of the urgent" to consume them. They don't think in terms of greatest impact. Instead, they think about surviving the week.

I was having lunch one day with a small group of pastors, sharing how they could mobilize more of their congregation into ministry. As I was talking about the Destiny Stage, it was as if a light bulb went off inside of one of the pastors who happened to be a worship leader. He relayed how just the day before, he had received an invitation from a friend to come to Mexico and train worship leaders who were gathering from across that country. I imagine that this pastor first viewed the request as a ministry interruption; after all, he would be gone from his congregation for several days. But as we talked about the Destiny Stage, he began to see this invitation not as an interruption, but as an opportunity to multiply his ministry. He could still faithfully serve the church God had called him to in the U.S. and make an impact abroad through multiplication.

Although I had done many leadership trainings around the world, the reality of multiplication really hit me while I was in Nigeria a few years ago. I was teaching 200 pastors and key church leaders who had gathered from all across that vast country. They hung onto every word that I and the other trainers with me said. They were writing notes just as fast as they possibly could. In fact, we had run out of time at the end of the conference before completing all of the points of a particular presentation. The people lined up afterward, pen and paper in hand, begging us to give them all of the information. I had no doubt that these highly motivated leaders who had listened so intently were going to take our teaching and use it to train people in their own churches. It may have looked like we were speaking to 200 people, but in reality, we were ministering to at least 20,000—the people those 200 would impact.

Through those 200 people, our ministry would now spread across that nation, including into staunch Muslim-controlled regions where I probably would never be able to go. That is multiplication! It is not about what I can accomplish alone, but what I can see accomplished by pouring myself into others. The Apostle Paul instructed Timothy, his missionary-protégé-turned-pastor, to "entrust to reliable men who will also be qualified to teach others" (2 Tim. 2:2). This is leveraging a few people to impact many.

What is *your maxpoint*? If you haven't reached it, do you have an idea what it might look like? If you find yourself in the Decision or Discovery stages, you probably don't have any idea what it looks like. You may not even know if you are in the Deployment Stage. That's okay! I believe that as we advance through these stages, our *maxpoint* comes into clearer focus. The important thing is that we are progressing in our walk with and service to Christ and that we are dreaming about becoming all that God would have us to become.

You may be asking yourself, "What does a *maxpoint* look like, anyway?" There are at least five characteristics. First, a *maxpoint* is *broad*. It reaches beyond you and your immediate "world." Second, it is *impacting*. It makes a significant difference in people's lives. Third, it is *multiplication*. It touches others, who in turn, touch others. Next, it is *Kingdom oriented*. It is not focused on building an empire for yourself or even an organization for others. It is about advancing God's Kingdom—God's agenda. Finally, your *maxpoint* is *natural*. It is the embodiment of who you are and what you were created by God to be. It is as natural for you as breathing.

It is important to remember that you have to go through all four of the stages (Decision, Discovery, Deployment, Destiny) to come to your *maxpoint*, which occurs while you are in the Destiny Stage. It is also important to note that reaching your *maxpoint* does not mean that you have "arrived" in life. Your *maxpoint* is not the end. We must continue to grow, learn, and become more like Christ. That process lasts our entire life. Also, reaching your *maxpoint* does not mean that you won't struggle with issues addressed in earlier stages. In fact, just the opposite is true. Daily we must decide to live for Christ. We continually discover more about ourselves, the Lord, and how to better please Him. We deploy ourselves into service and regularly evaluate that deployment in light of the destiny that God has for us. And, it is certainly possible to digress in our journey. Many people do. We must heed the words of 1 Corinthians 10:12, "So, if you think you are standing firm, be careful that you don't fall."

As you move through the four stages to your *maxpoint*, you will notice that there is not necessarily a clear line between the stages. You usually don't go to bed one day in the Deployment Stage and wake up the next in the Destiny Stage. Rather, it is a transformation process that blurs the lines between stages. Also, that transformation process is unique to you. While I believe the *Maxpoint* stages are universal, the process God uses to grow people through them, as well as the specific manifestation of the *maxpoint*, is different for each person.

A person may leave one position to reach his or her *maxpoint* in another position, while the person who replaced him or her finds their *maxpoint* in *that* position. Roy Frady, for example, had to *leave* Hollywood to pursue his *maxpoint* in vocational ministry. Yet I know of a vocational evangelist who left his circuit of churches to pursue his *maxpoint in* Hollywood. His daughter starred in a long-running TV sitcom. He moved to Hollywood to be near her and to impact that industry. Now he leads outreach Bible studies for those in TV and film. He also does work as an "extra" where he plays—of all things—a preacher! But he doesn't just act the part; he actually preaches the gospel of Jesus Christ. In one movie, he appeared in a scene for just a minute or two. To film that scene, however, the director needed him to "act" for an hour like he was preaching. He did, and as a result, several people working on the set gave their lives to Christ that day!

Todd Szalkowski left the business world to pursue his *maxpoint* in missions. Yet people like Norm Miller, Chairman of Interstate Batteries, saw his *maxpoint* in business. Miller uses his position and resources to impact lives ranging from workers at Interstate's Dallas headquarters, to the 200,000 dealers of their batteries around the world. Several years ago, Miller hired a full-time chaplain to minister to the Interstate staff and to coordinate funding efforts to various ministries.

Reaching your *maxpoint* is not about attaining a certain job position; rather, it is about becoming a certain kind of person who allows God to place him or her in the position that will bring God the greatest glory. It is not about going to a particular place, but about placing yourself where God wants you. When I go to Nigeria or any of the other countries where I minister, I am obeying Christ's command to go "to the ends of the earth." But what is the "ends of the earth" to me is actually the backyard of someone else! To a Nigerian, my Texas neighborhood would probably seem like the "ends of the earth." The objective is not to try and duplicate someone else's experience or calling, but to become all that God would have you to become as His unique creation.

Think about it ...

Have you become complacent about your spiritual and ministry growth?

What specific things are you doing to develop your life?

When was the last real step of faith that you took for God?

If you keep doing what you are doing now, will you reach your *maxpoint*?

Chapter 9
Sustaining the Point

The National Basketball Association (NBA) has some of the greatest dynasties of any sport. The Boston Celtics owned the court in the late 1950s and '60s, led by five-time MVP Bill Russell. They won the championship 11 times between 1957 and 1969, including an incredible eight consecutive years between 1959 and 1966. The most number of championships any other team had won in a row is three. The old Milwaukee Lakers did it between 1952 and 1954. The Chicago Bulls did it twice, first between 1991 and 1993 and again from 1996 to 1998. The Los Angeles Lakers accomplished a "three-peat" from 2000 to 2002. Even though they won three championships in a row at the beginning of this century, the Lakers were really the team to beat in the 1980s. They appeared in eight championship series, winning five. The Bulls dominated the decade of the 1990s, winning top honors six times.[11]

It is one thing for a team to win a season. It is quite another to sustain that winning momentum over a decade like the Celtics, Lakers, and Bulls have done. Ask any coach or player who has participated in one of these dynasties and he will tell you that maintaining that caliber

---

[11] Source: NBA.com.

of play is not easy. It takes an enormous amount of work, both on and off the court. But if you look deeper, you probably will see fundamental reasons why winners are winners.

Sustaining your *maxpoint*, like building a sport dynasty, is challenging. We have seen the incredible obstacles that all of us face, regardless of which journey stage we have reached. The pressures of society, peers, and our own pride, coupled with a minefield of temptations, can easily hinder a successful mission. Just because you reach the championship game one season doesn't mean you are guaranteed to stay there year after year. There are some winning fundamentals that must be present if you are going to sustain that level of operation. To bring that point home, let's take some pages out of the playbook of the man who epitomizes what it means to sustain your *maxpoint*: the Apostle Paul.

Paul certainly experienced many spiritual wins. He would tell you that the biggest one occurred while he was en-route to Damascus. It was the moment he was born again. Over the next few years, Paul moved through the Discovery Stage and entered the Deployment Stage, which occurred when he began ministering with Barnabas in Antioch. After a period of time, the vibrant Antioch Church sent Barnabas and Paul off on the first-ever organized missionary journey.

It appears that early in this trip, Paul reached his *maxpoint*, a place that he would successfully sustain for the rest of his life. It was at their first stop, the island of Cyprus, where Paul came into his own. Up to this point, Paul had a good ministry that had touched many lives. He had been operating in the Deployment Stage, effectively working with the Gentiles at Antioch in accordance with God's calling as the Apostle to the Gentiles. In a sense, however, Paul ministered under the shadow of Barnabas. Prior to Cyprus, the Book of Acts refers to the team as "Barnabas and Paul." From Cyprus forward, the focus shifts from Barnabas to Paul. The impact of Paul's ministry broadened greatly as God took it to a whole new level.

What is truly amazing about Paul is his longevity. Unlike Gideon, he did not fizzle. He sustained his *maxpoint* and departed this life as a truly mighty warrior for Christ. When we first glance at Paul, it is easy to feel intimidated. *I could never be like that,* we tell ourselves. Just like Michael Jordan was almost super-human on the basketball court, Paul was super-human in life. Yet, if we take a deeper look at Paul, we may be surprised to find some very practical, down-to-earth strategies that led to his spiritual success. We may not be able to hit a 30-foot, fall-away jumper at the buzzer to win the game like Jordan has done, but we can — through the power of God — sustain our *maxpoint*.

There are at least 57 passages in Paul's writings where he gives insight into sustaining his *maxpoint*. These truths fall into three categories, which we could consider as Paul's winning ingredients. They are attitude, actions, and approach to ministry. These were the fundamentals that Paul mastered for longevity in ministry.

Motivational speaker Zig Ziglar said that your attitude determines your altitude. How high you go in life is directly linked to your attitude. Look at a championship team and what is the first thing you see? You see attitude — a winning attitude. Paul's attitude was the backbone to everything in his life. It structured his life and held it together regardless of the circumstances in which Paul found himself at any moment. The right attitude can do the same for us.

The cornerstone of Paul's winning attitude was his attitude about himself. When he looked into the mirror, what did he see? He saw a slave (Ro. 1:1, 6:19; 1 Cor.4:1). Iosif Tson, speaking to a group in Dallas, said one of the biggest problems with the American church is that it has substituted the word *servant* for the world *slave* in its vocabulary. He pointed out that most English translations of the New Testament translate as *servant* the Greek word *doulos,* which is more accurately understood as *slave*. There are many books that talk about *servant* leadership. We hear plenty of preachers talking about how we should better *serve* Christ. After all, *serve* is a "nice" word. An employee *serves* his or her customer. The cook *serves* the meal. A servant may work for you today, but tomorrow decide to serve someone else if he or she makes him a better offer.

Contrast that with the word *slave*. Have you read any good books lately about *slave* leadership? Have you listened recently to radio sermons exhorting you to be a better *slave* for Christ? The connotation of the word *slave* is much stronger than *servant,* and honestly, it is not a very pretty word. If you are a slave, there is no possibility of leaving for greener pastures. You don't have a choice whether you will serve. You can't "take it or leave it." A slave is a slave regardless of his or her circumstances. Paul did not get up each morning and wrestle with whether he was going to serve Christ that day. Paul considered himself a slave of Christ. There was nothing with which to wrestle.

The slave attitude came easily for Paul, because he also considered himself dead (2 Cor. 4:7-12, 6:4-10). If you were a dead man walking, then you too would welcome the chance to be a slave. After all, if you are dead, there is no need to worry about how you feel or what your rights are. Paul looked in the mirror and saw a dead man. He was dead to himself. He had been crucified with Christ. "Paul" didn't exist anymore; it was only Christ who was alive.

I didn't notice John when he came into the retreat center during our monthly staff chapel. We often had guests, so seeing an unfamiliar face or two was not unusual. I did notice he remained seated while the rest of us were standing for our praise time. When we finished singing, John was introduced. He wasn't just a guest that day, he was a guest speaker. He made his way to the front of the audience, where he promptly sat down. I guessed John to be in his late 40s, although I can't recall him ever telling his age. He began to share his testimony. He was a successful businessman who had started several companies. He loved Christ and tried to let that love shine into his business practices. John told of a daughter who was in the midst of a long-term battle with an eating disorder. He told how this disorder had nearly taken her life. His eyes filled with tears as he shared his and his wife's despair over their daughter. Then he told us something else: He was dying. He had Lou Gehrig's disease, and the hourglass on his life was running out of sand. John was a walking dead man. Each day, life got a little bit harder. Each day, death got a little bit closer.

John described what it was like to be a dead man walking (although he did not use that term). As I sat there on the edge of my seat, eyes riveted on this fairly tall man, it was as if John pulled back the curtain on Heaven and gave us a guided tour. Seminary did not come close to giving me the insight into Heaven that this man did. Not surprising, since John seemingly had one foot there and one foot here. As you can imagine, the reality of impending death dramatically changed how John approached life. He saw everything differently. The things that once bothered him now seemed trivial, and he was more zealous in witnessing for Christ. As John faced physical death, he learned what Paul had learned: how to be dead to himself yet alive to Christ. This is what happens when you see yourself as dead.

Paul not only saw himself as a slave and as a dead man, he also considered himself a reflection of God (2 Cor. 3:18) and an unworthy recipient of God's grace (1 Cor. 15:9-10). He saw others as more important than himself (1 Cor. 10:33). In addition, he considered his weaknesses actually to be his strengths because it was those things that caused him to best depend on Christ (2 Cor. 12:10).

Paul also had a wonderful attitude about Christ. He longed to see Christ (2 Tim. 4:8) and considered Him to be preeminent in all things, making Him worthy of exaltation (Phil. 1:20-26, 3:7-9). Christ was the only place for Paul's confidence (Phil. 3:3-6), a fact about which he was never ashamed (Ro. 1:16). His "Christ first" attitude affected how he viewed material possessions. Possessions were a trust from God (1 Cor. 4:12) to use for the advancement of his life and ministry, but he would not allow them to possess him (1 Cor. 7:31). Because Paul maintained this philosophy, he was content with whatever he had at the moment, no matter how little or how much (Phil. 4:12-13).

We cannot leave the subject of Paul's attitude without pausing to consider his position toward suffering. It is an understatement to say that Paul knew what it was like to suffer physically and emotionally for Christ. It is difficult to imagine what it was like to have been beaten, stoned or to survive a shipwreck. I once saw a videotape of Christians in Iran being stoned to death, which as I understand it, is a regular event broadcasted on national television. It was horrific. This was Paul's plight.

I think about how Paul went through that incredible ordeal and still sustained his *maxpoint*. Paul viewed suffering as a gift from God (Phil 1:29) that would allow him to know Christ better (Phil. 3:10; 1 Cor. 4:9-13; Gal. 6:17) and express his faith (2 Tim 1:12). Paul's attitude, in general, was that his life was all about Christ (Gal. 2:7) and needed to be kept in perspective to eternity (2 Cor. 4:18).

The second section of Paul's playbook was his approach to ministry. All Christians should be in ministry, whether or not they get "paid" for it. With Amos, we saw that we should not be timid about attempting things for God even if we don't think we would be very good at them. Paul probably wasn't the greatest preacher to watch or listen to (Remember Eutychus in Acts 20:9 who fell asleep during one of Paul's long sermons? He dropped to the ground from the third story window where he had been sitting.), but he did not let his weaknesses keep him from attempting ministry (2 Cor. 10:6, 20).

Paul was people-focused, not program-focused, in his approach to ministry (Ro. 1:11-12, 16:1-15; Col. 1:28-29, 2:2). He took a team approach, involving others in his ministry (Ro. 15:30-31, 16:1-4; Eph. 6:19-20; Phil. 4:12-19; Col. 4:3-4; Philemon 7; see also his missionary journeys in the Book of Acts). We often think of Paul as a Lone Ranger, but the reality is he usually ministered with a team. He also kept things in perspective (Ro. 14:14-21; Phil. 1:12-14), and he adopted a "whatever it takes" approach to get the job done (1 Cor. 9:1-23; Phil. 1:15-18, 4:12-19).

Paul led by example (Phil. 3:17, 4:9), especially as he maintained integrity in ministry (2 Cor. 10:20). He was confrontational with people when necessary (1 Cor. 4:21), but he also "stopped to smell the flowers," as he took enjoyment of the ministry (Phil. 1:7; 1 Thes. 2:19). Pausing to enjoy the fruit of your labor is important. It is refreshing and encouraging. It often is the fuel that will keep you going when faced with challenging times or difficult people. When I was a pastor, I had a drawer in my desk where I kept thank-you notes and other encouraging letters that parishioners had given me. I often would pause in my busy day to go back and read them. They reminded me why I was doing what I was doing. They encouraged me that I was really making a difference in people's lives. They gave balance to the negative notes that also made their way to my desk! Although not one to spend much time reliving the past, I have found it helpful from time to time to review photos or reports from past ministry projects. Ministry is good, and it feels good to pause and reflect on its victories.

When I first met Iosif Tson many years after this Romanian had influenced my surrender to Christ's global calling, I told him about the impact he had on my life as a college student. "Stories like this are what keep an old preacher like me going," he replied. Well, stories also keep younger preachers and servants of Christ going!

The final part of Paul's winning strategy was simply his day-to-day actions. A good coach will tell you that sustained winning does not come from making big plays. It comes from consistently doing the little things right, which usually cause the big plays. Solomon tells us that it is the "little foxes that spoil the grapes." It is what we do day in and day out that will determine what we will become. It is proving ourselves faithful in the small things so we can be qualified for larger responsibilities.

Paul exercised great personal discipline by transforming his will to God's (Ro. 12:2), so that he could guard his actions (1 Cor. 6:12, 9:27; 2 Cor. 1:12), thoughts (2 Cor. 10:5; cf. 2 Cor. 10:3-6), and boasting (2 Cor. 10:13). He sought the praise of God each day, not of men (1 Thes. 2:4-6). He also made it his choice to forgive others as they wronged him (2 Tim. 4:16) and maintained a clear conscience from wronging God or others (2 Tim. 1:3).

Paul had two additional qualities that are present in every sports dynasty: the desire for more victories and the ability to make the most of each moment. Paul continually sought more fruit, never resting on his successes (Ro. 1:13). He was never satisfied with the status quo or with running a maintenance ministry. He wanted more. One of the saddest things I have noticed about many churches around the world is their contentment with the way things are.

They don't want to "rock the boat." They don't want to attempt anything new for God. They are happy in their comfort zone keeping things just the way they like it. If there was anyone "justified" in kicking back and cruising the twilight years of his life, it would have been Paul. But no, Paul would not stand for that.

Tony Evans once preached a great sermon about driving while looking in the rear-view mirror. If you are always looking backward, you never see what is ahead. It is okay periodically to glance in the rear-view mirror — it gives perspective, but you can't stare at it. Paul knew this, and so do all sports dynasties. You cannot win today's game by talking about the good 'ole days. You have to seize the opportunities that you have right now. Paul lived for the moment, not for what had happened yesterday (Phil. 3:12-14). Even if what happened in the past was awesome, it was still in the past. Yes, we can reflect on it and be encouraged by it, but we must move forward. Today is a new book with blank pages just waiting to be colored. Make the most of it!

Our attitude, our approach to ministry and our daily actions will determine whether we will sustain our *maxpoint*. They will tell us if our life will be a single winning season or a long-term winning dynasty. It is wonderful to reach our *maxpoint*, but it is far better to sustain it. Our journey is not a sprint; it is an ultra-marathon. So let's run with patience the race that is set before us.

Think about it ...

Are you building a godly dynasty with your life?

What is your attitude about yourself? Christ? What about suffering?

Do you take a people-focused or a program-focused approach to ministry?

Chapter 10
It's Looking Better All the Time

Peter Jenkins found himself disillusioned with life. The time was the mid-1970s. As Jenkins surveyed his affluent hometown of Greenwich, Connecticut, he decided there must be more to life than income and social status that characterized his city, which was then comprised of 60,000 people. So, this college grad decided he could find his answers by embarking, along with his dog Cooper, on a 5,000-mile trek across America.

In his now classic book, *A Walk Across America*, Jenkins tells how he frequently was asked what he was doing by people he met along the journey. The question was posed to him by a country doctor. Jenkins responded, "I'm walking across America. I started in upper New York state in October, and I'm heading down through the Deep South and then over to the West Coast." The doctor asked him why he would want to do such a thing. "To get to know the country," Jenkins responded. "So how does everything look?" the doctor asked. "You know, doc," Jenkins replied, "it's looking better and better all the time."[12]

Jenkins' words could be echoed for our journey. As the old gospel song says, "It gets sweeter as the days go by,"

---

[12] Jenkins, P. "A Walk Across America." *San Francisco: Perennial* (2001); page 2.

the more we get to know our Savior, the more profound our appreciation and love for Him become. We also grow to appreciate the marathon we are running. It is because of God's deep love for us that we are given the opportunity to experience His grace, not only in salvation but also in daily living.

If you have gone on a long car ride, you know how good it feels when you see a sign telling you how many miles it is to your destination. Each subsequent sign tells you that you are making progress. These signs are progress points that let you know where you are in your journey. Each one assures you that you are heading in the right direction. With that said, here are 10 progress points to ponder as we journey to our *maxpoint*.

Progress Point #1: You have taken the first step.

If you are a young or immature Christian, the concept of a *maxpoint* may seem too distant or be too overwhelming. Don't worry about that. Just take the next step that God has placed in front of you. Be faithful to what you know you are to do today, and face tomorrow when it arrives. If you have been walking with the Lord for some time, the question is, "What is the next step?" What is the next natural step God would have me take in my spiritual progression?

Progress Point #2: You have broken out of your comfort zone.

You have discovered that you must leave your comfort zone to get to your *maxpoint*. Abraham taught us this. He moved out of a geographic, cultural, and family comfort zone to experience God's blessings. When his journey started, he did not know where he was headed. It may have been a little scary at first, but that was okay, because God was doing the leading. Abraham believed God. However, remember that we can easily exchange one comfort zone for another if we are not careful. In any stage in the journey we are susceptible to getting stuck. Never let yourself get so comfortable that you cannot keep moving.

Progress Point #3: You are learning to maximize every situation.

Don't spend your time daydreaming about grass being greener somewhere else. Bloom where you are planted. That is what Joseph did. He did not wait for the next opportunity; he made the most of his current situation, seeing even the darkest of circumstances as an opportunity to excel.

Progress Point #4: You are maintaining your focus.

The author of Hebrews implores us to "fix our eyes on Jesus, the author and perfecter of our faith" (Hebrews 12:2). Like a lighthouse was to ships sailing in dense fog, so is the Lord Jesus to us on our journey. He is the compass that keeps us headed toward true north. Moses kept his focus on God, which is how he was able to overcome the constant grumbling, criticisms, and lack of faith of those around him. We should do the same. Life is full of distractions and potential detours. We cannot afford to get sidetracked by them. Life is too short!

Progress Point #5: Your faithfulness is being rewarded.

Christianity is not, "pie in the sky, sweet by and by, wait until you die." Yes, there are awesome rewards to come, but Jesus came to give us abundant life right now. Furthermore, we discover, like Joshua did, that if we will walk humbly before the Lord, He will exalt us at the right time. We learn, like Paul, to take joy from the fruit of our labor. There are many struggles in life, but we are able to bask in the glow of the goodness of God. We are able to experience that abundant, fulfilled life right now.

Progress Point #6: You are quick to flee from sin.

Nothing is more destructive to our successful mission than sin. There are enormous pressures on us from society, our peers, and even our own pride that place alluring temptations in our path. We are destined for failure if we try fighting sin on our own. Only through Christ will we be victorious. Christ in us is greater than he that is in the world. We should walk in wisdom, seeking to avoid temptations.

Progress Point #7: You are teachable.

People listened to Samuel because he first listened to God. Amos boldly stood up to wicked Amaziah because he first heard from God. Do you want to impact others? Do you want others to listen to you? Then you must first listen to the Lord. We also need to learn to listen to the constructive criticisms and advice given to us by others, just like Moses did. A teachable spirit is critical for growth and progress. No matter our age, none of us has yet arrived. There is always something more we can learn. There is always another lesson God wants to teach us. We are perpetual students.

Progress Point #8: You are attempting great things for God.

It was William Carey, the father of modern missions, who said, "Expect great things from God, attempt great things for God." Carey practiced what he preached by leaving his comfortable parish in England for the hardships of India. The Apostle Paul did not settle for the status quo, and neither should we. The deeper into the journey we get, the more opportunities come our way to make a real impact for Christ. We must take advantage of them. At times, this requires taking a risk. But after all, isn't that what faith is all about anyway? It is taking a risk by hoping in things you cannot see. It is taking a risk by going to the edge of everything you know and taking one more step into the unknown as you follow God's lead.

Progress Point #9: You give attention to the little things.

Winning teams win because they have mastered the fundamentals. The daily discipline of our thoughts, actions, and attitude will keep us from tripping, as we wind our way down life's path. What really makes or breaks our journey is not the major decisions of life, but rather the small, daily ones. If we consistently make the right decision in small things, the big decisions will take care of themselves. This attention applies to decisions and relationships. Remember, forgiveness is a powerful ally in life. It is critical to reaching and sustaining our *maxpoint*.

Progress Point #10: You keep fresh your love relationship with God.

Great relationships don't just happen, they take effort—lots of it. The same is true of our relationship with God. Meet with Him first thing each day, before you launch into your busy schedule. Talk with Him throughout the day. Seek His wisdom as you weigh your decisions by considering what would please Him. Never lose your first love! Do whatever it takes to maintain a vibrant relationship with the Lord.

You and I have the wonderful privilege of glorifying God with our lives and making His name known among those who have not experienced Him. Life is about so much more than simply hanging on for Heaven. It is about a beautiful journey which navigates us through the Decision Stage, launches us into the place of Discovery, lifts us into the orbit of Deployment, and then brings us to our *maxpoint* before we depart for the glorious and eternal place of deliverance. Walking with Christ is an incredible adventure, not to be missed by anyone! When you come to the final days of your life, do you want it said that you simply hung in there and made it? Or would you rather it be said that you faithfully served Christ in such a way that you made a broad and lasting impact?

The Psalmist instructs us, "Taste and see that the Lord is good." (Psalm 34:8). The more of Him we taste, the more we understand His goodness. But if we don't ever taste, then we will never see. Make the most of the life God has given you. Take God at His word and keep moving forward with Him. Then you can say of your life, "It's looking better and better all the time."

Resources

- Seminars, keynote messages, consulting, and other personal appearances by Frank Banfill

- *The MAXPOINT Journey Conference* — a fast-paced and biblical one-day conference designed to free people to thrive — not just survive — in life and ministry. Bring this exciting conference to your city, church, or ministry.

- Mobilization Campaigns — an eight-week church-wide emphasis to mobilize more people into service

- Personal and small group Bible study guides

- Books, CDs, and additional resources

- Bulk copies of this book at discounted prices

- *MaxPoint* for business and non-profit organizations — employee training and organizational development

For information on any of the above, please contact:

MaxPoint
311 N. Ballard Ave.
Wylie, TX 75098
(972) 429-6645
www.maxpoint.org

We Want to Hear from You!

Do you have a story you would like to share about how this book has impacted your life, your church or a friend? Please, send it to us at:

stories@maxpoint.org